CREATING A TWIST

fore

(

Other How To Books on Successful Writing

Copyright & Law for Writers
Creating a Twist in the Tale
Creative Writing
How to Be a Freelance Journalist
How to Master Business English
How to Publish a Book
How to Publish a Newsletter
How to Start Word Processing
How to Write a Press Release
How to Write a Report
How to Write an Assignment
How to Write an Essay
How to Write & Sell Computer Software
How to Write Business Letters
How to Write for Publication
How to Write for Television
How to Write Your Dissertation
Starting to Write
Writing a Non-fiction Book
Writing Reviews
Writing & Selling a Novel
Writing & Selling Short Stories

Other titles in preparation

The How To Series now contains more than 150 titles in the following categories:

Business Basics
Family Reference
Jobs & Careers
Living & Working Abroad
Student Handbooks
Successful Writing

Please send for a free copy of the latest catalogue for full details (see back cover for address).

SUCCESSFUL WRITING

CREATING A TWIST IN THE TALE

How to write winning short stories
for women's magazines

Adèle Ramet

How To Books

Cartoons by Simon Ramet

British Library Cataloguing in Publication Data

A catalogue record for this book is available from the British Library.

First published in 1996 by How To Books Ltd, Plymbridge House,
Estover Road, Plymouth PL6 7PZ, United Kingdom. Tel: Plymouth
(01752) 202301. Fax: (01752) 202331.

Note: The material contained in this book is set out in good faith for
general guidance and no liability can be accepted for loss or expense
incurred as a result of relying in particular circumstances on statements
made in this book. The law and regulations may be complex and liable to
change, and readers should check the current position with the relevant
authorities before making personal arrangements.

Produced for How To Books by Deer Park Productions.
Typeset by Concept Communications (Design & Print) Ltd, Crayford, Kent.
Printed and bound by The Cromwell Press Ltd, Broughton Gifford, Melksham,
Wiltshire.

Contents

List of Illustrations

Foreword

As Fiction Editor of *Bella* Magazine, I have been dealing with twist-ending stories for over eight years now and I know they bring an enormous amount of pleasure to a vast number of readers worldwide.

It takes a special skill to produce this work. In addition to an ability to tell a story that misleads the reader without cheating, the writer should have a devious, calculating but subtle approach to life and its problems!

As I am sure you will already have discovered, twist-enders are not easy to write but there is a big and growing market for them, so it is well worth persevering – from both your point of view and mine.

There is, as yet, no prize, no 'Booker' for authors who tackle these fiendishly difficult tales but when you have one accepted you join a very special club of writers who can be immensely proud of their work.

This book acknowledges that twist-enders are slightly different from other short stories and the art of writing them needs to be studied. I welcome it and hope that many of you who read on will soon be joining the ranks of the authors who tease, infuriate and, most of all, entertain us every week.

Linda O'Byrne
Fiction Editor, *Bella* magazine

Preface

DEFINING THE TWIST IN THE TALE

Writing twist-in-the-tale stories is easy. Or so many short story writers would have you believe. I have heard the twist technique dismissed as 'Simply a matter of leaving out a vital piece of information which is revealed right at the end', but nothing could be further from the truth.

If it is your intention to learn how to write twist stories for publication then this book will help to dispel some of the myths surrounding the techniques involved and set you on the right, albeit twisted, road to writing a short story with a twist in its tail.

Twist stories generally fall into two main categories, those in which the characters are not who or what they appear to be and those in which a devious central character receives his or her come-uppance. They may, of course, contain an element of both of these concepts but the ultimate goal is to totally mislead the reader into believing the image you wish to portray. However, if the twist is to be successful, the story must be carefully constructed so that the reader is completely happy with the surprise ending.

Magazine twist stories are very short, from as little as 500 words for some markets, and with such limited room for character development and atmospheric description, it is not surprising that the uniformed story writer tends to dismiss twists as pale imitations of the real thing.

However, the one thing a twist in the tale most definitely is not is a poorly planned story, with shallow characters and a flashy, trick ending. This approach only serves to make the reader feel cheated. In fact, the success of these stories depends upon the writer's ability to draw the reader into every twist and turn as the storyline develops.

This book is designed to introduce writers who may already have a working knowledge of fiction writing to the specialised requirements of writing twist stories.

Before the twist author sits down to write a story, he or she always knows exactly how it is going to end. This ability to write backwards, that is, working the story back from the ending, is just one of a number of techniques we will be exploring, illustrated by case studies and practical exercises.

Thanks are due to Linda O'Byrne, Fiction Editor of *Bella* magazine, for her invaluable support not only in the writing of this book but also in the development of my twisted mind.

ACKNOWLEDGEMENTS

In addition to Linda O'Byrne, I would like to thank Christine Hall of 'Scriptease Editorial' and authors Joyce Begg, Fred Clayson, Elizabeth Evans and Marion Naylor for their greatly valued assistance in the writing of this book.

I would also like to thank the following magazine editors for their helpful contributions:

The Editor, *Eva*
Lucy Bulmer, Deputy Editor, *Prima*
John Dale, Editor, *Take A Break*
Beverly Davies, Fiction Editor, *The Lady*
Gaynor Davies, Fiction Editor, *Woman's Weekly*
Emma Fabian, Fiction Editor, *That's Life*
June Hammond, Editor, *Woman*
April Joyce, Fiction Editor, *19*
Linda Kelsey, Editor, *She*
Sinclair Matheson, Editor, *People's Friend*
Kati Nicholl, Fiction Editor, *Woman & Home*
Neil Patrick, Editor, *Yours*
Pat Richardson, Fiction Editor, *Best*
Sally Sheringham, Fiction Editor, *Woman's Realm*
Shelly Silas, Fiction Editor, *Chat*
Ian Sommerville, Fiction Editor, *My Weekly*

Adèle Ramet

1
Researching the Market

UNDERSTANDING THE MAGAZINE MARKET

Until the late 1980s, when German publishers H. Bauer and Gruner & Jahr brought their weekly publications *Bella* and *Best* to the UK, fiction for the women's magazine market had a distinctly romantic feel to it. 5,000-word romances and weekly serials could be found on the pages of most major titles, many of which featured a minimum of two stories a week.

The new German magazines were totally different from anything the UK readership had seen before. Gone were the lengthy romances bearing the editorial labels, 'poignant', 'heartwarming' or 'touching'. Gone, too, were the dramatic serialisations of family sagas and historical novels.

The 'village' style

With their gossipy but practical formats and short, snappy 'village' styles, *Bella* and *Best* offered a totally new concept to their target readership. Within a very short space of time, they had toppled their main rivals from the leading slots and caused a major revamp in the UK's established magazine market.

Compared to their British counterparts, the magazines were factual and fast-paced, offering an informative, easy read for busy, independent women aged from late teens upwards. The target audience was wide, encompassing working singles and stay-at-home mothers.

FOLLOWING THE FORMULA

Using a formula successfully tried and tested in the United States, the new magazines actively encouraged reader involvement. They invited readers' contributions for a variety of features, 'true life confessions' and advice columns, welcoming material from professional freelancers.

There was little room in the new magazines for the 'soap' stars and celebrities who dominated the pages of UK publications. The woman of the 1980s not only ran a home, she went out to work or returned to study. She was extremely mobile and this, in itself, enabled her to broaden her horizons. Following the fortunes of the rich and famous was all very well but the Germans had caught on to the fact that 1980s woman wanted to read about people whose achievements she could really relate to.

Television soaps

Around the time that these magazines were taking off in the UK, the TV soap *Neighbours* was hitting our television screens. Using the same gossipy format, the show was a runaway success, reinforcing the belief that the target audiences were far more interested in how the woman down the road coped when she discovered her husband in bed with her mother, than the love lives of arrogant and invariably ageing film actresses.

IDENTIFYING YOUR READERSHIP

With the emphasis firmly on their readership, lifestyle features revolved around ordinary homes that were instantly recognisable. Practical DIY columns conveyed the clear message that not every woman has or wants a man around. Tips on decorating the home, plumbing, rewiring and car maintenance appeared alongside the more familiar beauty pages, knitting patterns and cookery columns.

Empowering the reader

Informed self-help was the order of the day with information on healthcare, finance and consumer rights. Columns with titles like 'Job of the Week' or 'Woman of the Week' invariably featured 'ordinary' women who had either achieved success in a male-dominated environment or whose work was far removed from the stereotypical female careers of teacher, nurse or secretary.

The most noticeable change, however, was on the fiction pages. Although innovative for the time, *Bella* was perhaps slightly more conventional in featuring a two-page romantic story in addition to the one-page 'Mini Mystery'.

Best, however, had little time for romance in their practical commonsense format. Their '5 Minute Fiction' story was just that, a one-page twist story with no room for sentiment.

Working women

The image of the stay-at-home housewife with time to relax, put her feet up and become immersed in her favourite magazine was soon to become a thing of past. *Bella* and *Best* readers were perceived as belonging to the fast-moving world of the commuter or busy working mother. The magazines were designed to be read travelling to work on the train or during coffee and lunch breaks. This on-the-move image was reflected in the twist stories, which offered a quick complete read to its active target group.

Sweeping changes in fiction

The influence these two publications have had on today's women's magazine market should not be underestimated. During the intervening eight or so years, popular weeklies such as *Woman* and *Woman's Realm* have adopted much of the format introduced by the German publications and possibly the most sweeping of all the changes can be found on the fiction pages with the inclusion of the one-page twist in the tale.

MEETING DIFFERENT DEMANDS

In the struggle to maintain circulation figures, revamps in both content and style are constantly taking place. Twist stories have shortened from around 1,400 words to between 1,000 and 1,200 words. Even in magazines such as *My Weekly* which, despite competition from newcomers, continues steadfastly to feature the longer romances and serials, the twist in the tale has managed to gain a foothold, albeit confined to a 500-word half-page slot.

Catering for different age groups

UK titles which traditionally catered for the over-forties have found to their cost that the mature reader prefers a gentle approach. Having adopted the twist format and found it successful, the stories still have a place in these publications but the emphasis tends to be rooted in romance with its mandatory happy ending.

Indeed, in some magazines, the twist is almost imperceptible as today's fiction editors strive to achieve that elusive 'feel good factor' for which 1990s woman apparently yearns. One thing is for sure, however, even though its hard edge may have softened, the twist-in-the-tale short story is here to stay.

Revamping the formula

The style and content of the original German magazines has also changed considerably over the years. Celebrities, apparently eager to show off the interiors of their luxury homes, have managed to creep back onto their pages, effectively ousting the no-nonsense, practical DIY and motoring features that typified these publications in their early days.

It would appear, too, that a readership battered by the harsh realities of a struggling economy, redundancy and broken relationships is currently displaying a preference for uplifting stories offering hope and escapism.

WRITING TO STYLE

In order to write effectively for the market, it is essential that you have in-depth knowledge of each publication's style, content and target readership. Not only must you have a good understanding of the age, lifestyle and probably income bracket of the readers but the magazine for which you have chosen to write must appeal to you personally as a 'good read' and feature characters with whom you can identify. If you are unfamiliar with the content and style of the magazine or have a patronising attitude to the readership, this will be immediately apparent in your work.

Analysing the magazine

Once you have selected a suitable publication, buy it regularly for a minimum of two months and study it in depth. A detailed analysis sheet similar to the one shown in Fig. 1 is well worthwhile, but for a rough guide, the following items will give you a clear picture of the target readership:

- Advertisements
- Reader's letters
- Cookery columns
- Fashion and beauty pages
- Agony column
- Travel pages
- Fiction pages

If the bulk of the advertisements are for footwarmers and stair lifts, with the letters pages sprinkled with anecdotes about grandchildren, then it's a safe bet that the publication is aimed principally at the mature reader. Similarly, if the travel pages are full of low-cost family packages, with

Magazine title ....

Editor/editorial address ....

....

Contents:	No. of columns/ page(s)	Average no. words per item
Advertisements	....	....
Agony column	....	....
Book/film/video reviews	....	....
Celebrity interviews	....	....
Competitions	....	....
Crafts	....	....
DIY	....	....
Fashion	....	....
Fiction	....	....
Finance	....	....
Food & Drink	....	....
Gardening	....	....
Health & Beauty	....	....
Horoscopes	....	....
Medical	....	....
Motoring	....	....
Patterns (knit/sew)	....	....
Pets	....	....
Readers' letters	....	....
Readers' true life tales	....	....
Special features	....	....
Special offers	....	....
The Arts	....	....
Travel	....	....
Other (specify)	....	....

Tick the categories catered for:

Teenagers ....Mothers with babies...............Grandmothers........

Working mothers ....Unskilled ....Professionals ....

Other (specify) ....

Age Range: ....

Target Readership: ....

Fig. 1. Magazine analysis sheet.

advice on how to keep small children occupied on long journeys, the editorial slant will be towards younger women. In each case, the fiction pages will reflect the lifestyle of the magazine's readership.

ANALYSING PUBLISHED STORIES

The main advantage of the twist story as far as the writer is concerned is that it fits neatly into most genres. For example, the basic 'girl meets boy' storyline can appear in a number of formats.

Fiction formats

- A romance where the reader is led to believe that the girl is disinterested when, in truth, she is allowing her man to chase her so that she can catch him.

- A ghost story in which one of the central characters is a spectre.

- A retribution story, where one or other or even both of the characters get their come-uppance.

- A psychological thriller where the girl could be throwing herself at a man the reader knows is a psychopath.

- A black comedy, where one character's attempts to murder the other are consistently thwarted in suitably amusing fashion by the unsuspecting prospective victim.

- A science fiction story in which one of the characters is an android. (Twist in the tale is the only format in which some women's magazines will accept futuristic settings.)

- A crime story where one of the characters has been double-crossed by the other.

- A lifestyle story in which the girl explores the changing nature of her current relationship.

- An historical story where, despite an apparently modern setting, the characters turn out to be a famous couple from the past, e.g. Cleopatra and Mark Anthony.

Flexibility

For the purposes of a magazine fiction writer, therefore, the twist in the tale is just about the most flexible short story form available. Not only can it be adapted to suit almost any genre but it also appeals to any age and social group.

However, in order to offer maximum reader identification, the characters in the stories must reflect the magazine's readership with regard to age, social attitudes and aspirations.

When analysing the fiction regularly featured in your chosen publication, look for the following points:

- the age of the characters
- the types of endings, e.g. happy, tough, serves 'em right, etc.
- the genres, e.g. ghost, thriller, lifestyle, romance
- the style, e.g. humorous, gentle, hard-hitting
- the length.

REQUESTING GUIDELINES

A brief, courteous letter to the fiction editor requesting editorial guidelines and enclosing the obligatory stamped self-addressed envelope will almost always result in a helpful reply.

SENDING UNSOLICITED MANUSCRIPTS

The best way to discover whether or not your manuscript is suitable for publication is to send it to a magazine editor. Manuscripts submitted in this way, 'on spec' or 'unsolicited', will usually be considered but be aware that not all fiction editors are prepared to look at uncommissioned work.

In these magazines, there will almost always be a note stating that 'We do not consider unsolicited fiction' underneath the editorial address and novice writers would be well advised to avoid sending material to them.

For published writers, it may be worth contacting the fiction editors of such publications direct with details of your previous writing experience as, in the light of this, you may then be asked to send samples of your work for consideration.

CASE STUDIES

Arthur tries his hand at fiction

Arthur is a recently retired bank clerk. His perception of the female role is that of housewife, cook and chatterbox. He can't understand what his wife occupies herself with all day as housework is, in his opinion, so undemanding.

He has written the occasional article for the bank's house journal and a cursory glance at his wife's weekly magazine convinces him that he should turn his talents to fiction. Despite the fact that he doesn't really want his name appearing in a publication for women, he believes he could easily write a suitable short story for it.

Sadly, Arthur's 10,000-word romance entitled 'Love is a Money Splendoured Thing – Confessions of a Retired Bank Clerk' and submitted under the pseudonym 'Violet Bedworthy' is rapidly returned to him. His patronising attitude and lack of empathy with the magazine's readership has come over loud and clear. So, too, has his lack of professionalism with regard to the length and style of his story.

Frank studies the market

Like, Arthur, Frank is recently retired. An avid reader, he thoroughly enjoys the weekly twist story featured in his wife's regular magazine.

After carefully studying the format, he comes up with an idea which he feels will appeal to the magazine's readership. He writes the story to the required length of 1,200 words and addresses it to the fiction editor by name with a brief covering letter and a stamped self-addressed envelope.

On this occasion, his story is rejected but is returned with a copy of the magazine's fiction guidelines and a request to see more of his work.

Frank studies the guidelines before writing several more stories, two of which are rejected but the rest are accepted. He now writes regularly for several women's magazines.

Selecting your market

We will be looking at presentation and marketing of manuscripts in a later chapter but in order to avoid making the same mistakes as Arthur, use the following checklist.

CHECKLIST

1. Do you enjoy reading the magazine from cover to cover?

2. Have you bought the magazine regularly for at least two months?

3. Do you identify with the readership?

4. Are you sure you can write to the magazine's housestyle?

5. Do you know the required length?

6. Have you obtained the fiction editor's name and correct editorial address?

7. Do you have a copy of the editor's fiction guidelines?

ASSIGNMENT

Purchase a selection of women's magazines and make a detailed written analysis of each one along the same lines as the questionnaire featured earlier in this chapter. Compare the results and you will gain a clear picture of the target readerships.

2
The Characters are the Story

BLENDING CHARACTERS AND STORY

What is a short story?

A short story can be defined as a significant incident or turning point in a fictional character's life. Without detailed knowledge of the character's personality or experiences, it will be impossible for you to know what kind of incident would prove to be significant for them.

Knowing your characters

One misconception about twist stories is that, as they are so short, there is no need to worry too much about the characterisation. In fact, in a twist in the tale, the characters *are* the story and must, therefore, be totally realistic.

Characters can be any age, from newborn babies to elderly pensioners. They may be stunningly beautiful or hideously ugly, highly intelligent or dimwittedly slow. Whoever and whatever they are, it is up to you, as their creator, to know them inside out.

When thinking about your character's appearance, remember that unlike the romantic hero, the twist story male need not be in his mid-thirties, well over six feet tall with thick, luxuriant dark hair and piercing blue eyes.

Our man can be short, fat, skinny or spotty and far from sporting a boyish mop of unruly hair, may well be a balding, middle-aged wimp with pudgy hands and a less than attractive personality.

Equally, heroines need have little or no feminine appeal. They can be plain or even downright frumpy because, for twist purposes, the better looking the women are, the more jealous and spiteful they tend to be.

In contrast to their romantic counterparts, characters in twist stories do not necessarily have exciting careers. Very often, the duller their existence, the better the story's twist, and whereas in romantic fiction the central character is invariably en route to power and fame, the twist story hero may simply be seeking a quiet life.

Once you have your characters clearly in your mind, set the details down in a brief CV (see Fig. 2).

Caring what happens

Equally important is the fact that you, the writer, must care what happens to your characters. Whether you intend to turn the tables on them or have them win through in the end, if you don't truly care about the outcome, neither will your reader.

Looks, personality, age all naturally have a bearing on the storyline and with so little room for lengthy descriptive passages, the majority of twist stories are set in the here and now, against instantly recognisable backdrops.

Finding suitable locations

Because they live and work in similar environments to the magazine's readership, twist characters tend to be very down-to-earth. The problems, inconveniences and irritations they encounter mirror their readers' own lives.

Whilst you will occasionally find exotic locations, luxurious homes and cosy country cottages in twist stories, these backgrounds are invariably used as a contrast to the cynical characters who inhabit them.

Avoiding stereotypes

One difficulty when writing about identifiable people set in familiar locations is that they may appear rather stereotypical. This can prove an asset in helping the writer set a scene effectively but clichéd characters must be avoided at all costs. In particular, ethnic or social stereotypes which reveal racist or similar prejudices on the part of the writer are totally unacceptable.

As a rule, twist characters lead humdrum lives in ordinary homes surrounded by apparently ordinary people. They are you and me, Mr and Mrs Average, struggling to win through against all the odds. Whether they achieve their aims or fail miserably in the attempt largely depends not upon the location, genre or lifestyle but on their personality and, of course, the twist in the tale.

To illustrate how characters fit into immediately identifiable backgrounds, match the characters (1–4) below to *your* perception of their natural setting (a–d):

1. A harassed young mother
2. A house-proud housewife

Age ....

Hair colour ....

Eye colour...

Height ....

Weight..

General appearance ....
(smart, scruffy, elegant, gawky, etc.)

Personality ....
(happy, sad, jolly, spiteful, etc.)

Education ....

Location ....

Living accommodation..

Occupation ....

Marital status ....

Background...

....

Past behaviour/experiences which would have a bearing on
your character's reactions to the current situation ....

....

....

....

Fig. 2. Sample CV format.

3. A secretive elderly couple
4. A shoplifter

(a) A retirement bungalow
(b) A large department store
(c) A cramped high-rise flat
(d) An immaculate three-bedroomed suburban semi

CHARACTERISING THROUGH NAMES

Names are incredibly useful tools in creating the image you wish to portray. Used correctly, they will give the reader a clear idea of the age, social status and personality of your character.

For example, a 'Jack' could be a bit of a lad, whilst a 'Jacob' might be rather staid and set in his ways.

Changing fashions

When deciding upon a name for your character, always take into account the fact that fashions change.

The name Jason, for example, used to be associated with young men from wealthy backgrounds. Today's Jason, however, is invariably a teenage tearaway. For girls, the name Daisy is currently making a comeback, but until recently it was an ideal name for a very old lady.

When deciding upon names for your characters, your own personal experiences and perceptions will play a major part in your final choice. The selection of names listed below should each convey to you a different age group and social type:

- Bert
- Gladys
- Piers
- Tracey
- Felicity
- Darren

SELECTING A VIEWPOINT CHARACTER

The number of characters in a short story should always be kept to an absolute minimum. Twist plots can be quite complex so it is sensible to avoid the unnecessary complication of superfluous characters. Whilst a skilful writer can cope with three or even four characters within a 1,200 word story the ideal number is, without doubt, **two**.

Functions of the viewpoint character

The viewpoint character is the one through whose eyes the story is told so he or she must perform the following functions:

- Be the character with whom your readership is most likely to identify.

- Portray the emotion you wish to convey.

- Provide the problem.

- Provide an element of suspense.

- Be the character most qualified to convey the author's message.

- Have the ability to offer a solution to the problem.

You can tell your story either in the first person, where the writer assumes the role of the 'I' or central character, or third person, where the writer is one step removed from the action by using the pronouns 'he' or 'she'.

For novice writers the first person, or 'I', viewpoint is often the most effective as it serves to involve the writer personally in the storyline, so helping to prevent a change of viewpoint halfway through.

PLAYING AROUND WITH FIRST AND THIRD PERSON

With so few characters to choose from and armed with the checklist above, selecting your viewpoint character should not pose too much of a problem.

Occasionally, however, the story takes over and before you know what has happened, you begin to lose empathy with your viewpoint character and transfer your sympathies to a minor one. If this should occur, you will need to stop and think again about your approach.

Changing the viewpoint character

The solution may simply be to change your viewpoint character or to switch from third to first person. To give you an idea of what can happen, we can select a character and location from the list given earlier in this chapter.

Sample storyline

Using a suburban semi-detached house as a background, we can have as our central character a housewife in her late thirties. We'll call her Audrey. She is neat, elegant and obsessively house-proud. She does not go out to work, nor does she have any children. She is comfortably off but not wealthy and appears to be perfectly content until her sister, Lynette, comes to stay.

Lynette is useless around the house, a contributory factor to her latest relationship breaking up. She has run to her older, sensible sibling for comfort but the two sisters have never really got on.

Stunningly beautiful, Lynette eats like a horse and never puts on an ounce, looking wonderful in leggings and a sloppy sweatshirt. Audrey is constantly dieting and wears nothing more casual than tailored slacks and chain-store blouses.

First person viewpoint

You may, initially, identify with Audrey and writing in the first person, begin with something along the following lines:

I knew if Lynette stayed in my house for one more day, I couldn't be held responsible for my actions.

However, let's assume that you suddenly find Audrey's obsession with housework extremely irritating. You would then become quite sympathetic towards Lynette and this would have a bearing on the twist in the tale. In order for the story to work, you would need to rewrite it from Lynette's viewpoint, opening with something like:

I do wish Audrey wasn't so fussy. I may not be house-proud like her but then, no one normal could be.

Third person viewpoint

When using first person viewpoint, however, you can only guess what is going on in the minds of the other characters and cannot follow them if they move out of sight or hearing.

Third person offers slightly more flexibility. You still tell the tale through your viewpoint character's eyes but you can give a clearer impression of the thoughts and actions of others in the story.

You can also take a more detached stance with third person, particularly if rather than sympathising with one of the sisters, you find that you dislike them both.

In third person, from Audrey's viewpoint, the opening might read as follows:

Aware that her sister was deliberately taunting her, Audrey waited irritably while Lynette slowly drained her drink. As soon as she saw Lynette set the glass down on the table, Audrey pounced on it, the back of her neck flushed red with temper.

SWITCHING VIEWPOINT

As previously mentioned, viewpoint switches invariably occur by accident when, as you write the story down, your sympathies towards the characters change. Switching viewpoint in this way always results in confusion and makes the story unworkable. It is, therefore, inadvisable ever to switch viewpoint in a short, twist story.

Exceptions to the rule

There are, however, always exceptions to any rule and one particular format does rear its head from time to time. This is when the central character is removed, either by death or by something similarly dramatic, usually in the penultimate paragraph. It then falls to another character to carry the story through to the end.

Applying this technique to our original storyline, the viewpoint would suddenly shift from Audrey to Lynette with something along the following lines:

Audrey's viewpoint

Audrey glared furiously at the glutinous mess embellishing the base of her non-stick frying pan. Lynette had gone too far this time. She wanted her out right now! But as she ran, fuming, to call her sister, Audrey lost her footing on the newly polished floor and smashing her head on the shining worksurface, fell lifelessly onto the gleaming tiles.

Viewpoint switch to Lynette

Upstairs, Lynette paused and listened for a brief instant before throwing the rest of her things into the holdall. If Audrey thought her childish crashing around in the kitchen bothered her, she was very much mistaken. Unaware of the pool of blood that was, at that very moment, spreading a red stain the length and breadth of Audrey's spotless vinyl, Lynette hurried down the stairs and slipping silently through the varnished front door, closed it firmly behind her.

Switching viewpoint with more than two characters

Another method sometimes used is that of switching viewpoint throughout the story from one character to another via a series of brief scenes. This technique requires a great deal of expertise to keep a thread running through the story which will bring all the characters together satisfactorily at the end.

Although very effective when it works, it should only be used if the writer is absolutely convinced that it will enhance and improve the basic storyline.

As a general rule, viewpoint switches are confusing for both the writer and the reader and best avoided in a twist in the tale.

CHECKLIST

1.   Do you know what motivates your central character?

2.   Do you care what happens to the character?

3.   Will the character put over the message you wish to convey?

4.   Does your character inhabit a realistic setting?

5.   Will your readership identify with the character?

6.   Have you switched viewpoint?

ASSIGNMENT

A recently divorced woman in her early forties goes to the bank with the intention of asking for a loan. The counter clerk, a twenty-year-old male trainee, is unable to help her but escorts her to the manager, a man in his late fifties.

During the ensuing conversation, the manager displays a sexist attitude towards his customer which conveys the impression that he disapproves of her divorced status and is scathing of her ability to manage her finances.

Select a viewpoint character from the three described above and using the checklist as a guide, write a scene between them, in first or third person, without switching viewpoint.

3
Action, Reaction and Interaction

COMBINING DIALOGUE AND ACTION

Analysis of twist stories from a selection of women's magazines will reveal a high proportion of dialogue in the text.

With a maximum length of around 1,200 words, the twist story writer is faced with the difficult task of setting the scene, characters and story-line in as few sentences as possible. One of the most effective ways to do this is through a combination of dialogue and action.

The functions of dialogue

Dialogue performs a number of vital functions:

- It describes the characters.
- It moves the story forward.
- It creates conflict, tension and suspense.
- It reveals background information.
- It conveys emotion.
- It sets the pace.

In addition to these functions, in a twist story, dialogue is used to help mislead the reader, a technique we will look at in more detail in Chapters 4 and 5.

Writing direct speech

When writing direct speech, try to avoid the use of 'he/she . . . said', 'asked', 'exclaimed', 'shouted', 'pleaded', 'expostulated', etc.

For example, at first glance, the passage below would seem to be per-fectly acceptable:

'Why can't you ever hang up your clothes?' asked Audrey, moving purposefully across the bedroom. 'I don't know how you can sleep in

*this mess,' she said irritably as she began to neatly smooth and fold
each crumpled item.*

However, by cutting out 'asked', 'said', 'as' and the extra 'she', we lose
four superfluous words and the piece flows much more smoothly:

> *'Why can't you ever hang up your clothes?' Audrey moved purpose-
> fully across the bedroom. 'I don't know how you can sleep in this
> mess.' Irritably, she began to neatly smooth and fold each crumpled
> item.*

Using dialogue alone

You can legitimately lose even more words by removing all the descriptive action within each conversation and writing in dialogue alone.
Knowing that, whilst Audrey is house-proud, Lynette is not, we can easily tell which one is speaking, as the following passage illustrates:

> *'Why can't you ever hang up your clothes? I'm sick and tired of pick-
> ing them up from this chair and putting them away for you.'*
> *'Leave them alone then, I never asked you to touch them. I can't
> stand it when you fuss around me all the time.'*

We can clearly identify the sisters' irritation with one another but
although the technique of using dialogue alone works well for short passages it becomes confusing if it is sustained throughout the whole story.

Bringing characters alive through their actions

The inclusion of action dramatically improves the pace and helps to
bring the story alive as you can see when we combine the previous
examples in the following way:

> *'Why can't you ever hang up your clothes?' Audrey moved purpose-
> fully across her sister's bedroom. 'I'm sick and tired of picking them
> up from this chair and putting them away for you.'*
> *'Leave them alone then,' Lynette shifted more comfortably against
> her pillows. 'I never asked you to touch them.' Absently, she inspect-
> ed her newly painted fingernails. 'I can't stand it when you fuss
> around me all the time.'*

The fact that Lynette's actions contradict what she is actually saying
leaves us in little doubt that she is perfectly happy to let Audrey put her

things away for her. The conversation also tells us that clearing up after her sister is nothing new for Audrey and so gives us more of an insight into their relationship.

Even though wordage is very tight it is, therefore, worth the extra words it takes to tell the story through a combination of both action and dialogue.

GRABBING THE READER'S ATTENTION

As previously mentioned, there is no space in magazine fiction for scene-setting and long, descriptive passages. Your opening sentence will have to convey as much of this information as possible whilst drawing the reader immediately into the story.

Opening a story with dialogue

Dialogue is one of the most frequently used methods of opening a story and is certainly one of the most effective. For example, the first paragraph of the above conversation would serve as a perfectly good opening to our story. It introduces the two main characters, giving you an idea of their relationship and their location.

Essential elements of an opening

It is by no means essential to begin with a line of dialogue but your opening must contain the following elements:

- a sense of time
- a sense of place
- a sense of movement.

Your central character must appear in the opening and should speak the first line of dialogue.

It is not necessary to set the scene – a short story begins at a point where something significant is about to happen. To illustrate how you simply dive straight into the action, set out below is a selection of opening lines from twist stories by published writers Joyce Begg, Fred Clayson and Marion Naylor:

> *Charles Teddington looked across the table at his wife and wondered, yet again, what it was that had made him decide to marry her all those years ago.*

> ('Still Waters', *Woman's Realm* 1993)

Late one evening, Bob Harris opened the envelope that he'd been ignoring all day, pulled out the contents and groaned, 'Another damned bill!'

('Breaking Even', *Bella* 1995)

Ken paused for a breather, holding the dripping paddle in the air, 'Nice bit of scenery,' he said complacently.

Daisy cast a jaundiced eye over the fog-shrouded Scottish hills and the sullen grey water, 'It's all right but I like a bit of life. Bright lights, plenty of company. Give me Glasgow any time. Where are we anyway?'

('Unnecessary Risk', Bella 1995)

The first impression of Joyce Begg's character, Charles Teddington, is that he is both arrogant and unpleasant. You are compelled to read on to find out more about him and his long-suffering wife.

The second example goes for immediate reader identification. Fred Clayson has used both action and dialogue to convey that familiar sinking feeling we all experience when a bill arrives on the doormat. We must read more if we are to discover how Bob Harris copes with his financial problems.

In the third opening, through a skilful combination of dialogue and action, Marion Naylor effectively sets the scene and the personality of her characters in a very few words. We know vaguely where and who they are but the only way we can find out what they are doing there is to keep on reading.

All three of these openings are highly effective in grabbing the reader's attention and pulling them into the story.

CHOOSING THE RIGHT VOCABULARY

Because you are so constrained by length in magazine twist stories, every word must be there for a purpose. The vocabulary you use must not only be evocative of the characters, their actions and surroundings, it must also reflect the everyday speech of your readership.

Avoiding long words

Some novice writers have a tendency to use long words in the misguided belief that they will impress their readers. In fact, complicated vocabulary slows down the pace and if used incorrectly, will make a nonsense of your work. If you feel a word is overlong or you are unsure of its meaning, cut it out.

Dialect is another problem area for the fiction writer. If it is essential to the storyline for a character to have a cockney accent, the odd dropped 'h' might just be acceptable but the last thing you want to do is hit the reader with a confusing mess of apostrophes and italicised words.

Achieving a realistic accent

The most effective way to achieve an accent is to let the rhythm of speech convey it for you.

In a story entitled 'Will Power' (*Bella* 1995) I included an Asian character called Mr Varma. His first line is 'Calm yourself, Miss Finch. *I'm sorry if I startled you.*'

Constructed in this way, it injected just the right lilt into his speech. Had he been cockney, the sentence would probably have read, '*Calm down, love. Sorry if I gave you a fright.*'

Vocabulary guidelines

The following guidelines will help you to assess whether your vocabulary is suitable for your chosen market:

● Know the true meaning of every word you use.

● Check that you have clearly said what you meant to say.

● Check that your dialogue sounds realistic.

● Make sure your dialogue is in character.

● Use dialect sparingly.

KEEPING THE STORY MOVING

Whilst magazine twist stories are designed to be a quick, easy read, the pace nevertheless depends upon the story's content and style.

Slowing and speeding the pace

Because they are so short, twist tales unfold extremely rapidly from start to finish. If, however, your story has a romantic theme or you wish to build up the tension, you may need to slow the pace down to achieve the desired effect.

As a rough guide, remember that short sentences speed up the pace, long ones slow it down, as you can see from the following examples:

1.   *The bus hurtled towards the ravine. A woman screamed. Brakes squealed. They shuddered to a halt.*

2.   *They drifted lazily along, waves gently lapping the side of the boat as it followed the course of the river, meandering peacefully towards the sleepy little hamlet.*

Note, too, the verbs and adverbs used to conjure up the desired picture. The bus 'hurtles' whilst the boat 'drifts lazily'.

Keeping the story moving

It has already been mentioned that twist stories work most effectively if they are told in the 'here and now'. However, this does not mean that you are metaphorically 'running on the spot'. You need to keep the story moving in order to carry your reader from the beginning to the final twist ending.

So far, our sisters Audrey and Lynette have not moved out of the bedroom. However, if we decide to keep the viewpoint switch ending used in Chapter 2, Audrey will have to make her way downstairs at some stage. She's already begun to argue with Lynette but we'll need to keep that going for a bit longer if we are to bring in all the necessary background information, build up the tension and set everything up for the final twist.

Short and snappy

The dialogue used for the row will be short and snappy, keeping up the impetus and ensuring that both sisters make their intentions clear, throwing in some references to past quarrels and injustices. However, the viewpoint stays with Audrey so we will need to follow her out of the bedroom and down the stairs to the kitchen.

Slowing the pace with description

We could slow things down a little at this point using description to convey Audrey's emotions. Maybe she feels that she's gone too far and wants to make amends. She could hurry to the top of the stairs but hesitate, descending slowly while she considers her next course of action. Perhaps she pauses at the kitchen door, delaying her entry and so building up the tension prior to her discovery of Lynette's latest misdemeanour.

The timespan of our story from start to finish will be less than half an hour. In that time, however, the reader must have learnt a great deal about the two women, their backgrounds and their relationship with one another. Having hooked our reader with an irresistible opening, if we've done our job properly, she or he will be unable to put the story down until the final twist is revealed.

RESPONDING REALISTICALLY TO UNUSUAL SITUATIONS

Whilst the behaviour of our central characters is dictated by their personalities and past experiences, we still need to provoke them into realistic reaction by setting them up to behave in a certain way.

Reacting to given situations

Our two sisters have been described in such a way that the reader can predict how they will react to a given situation. Knowing how house-proud Audrey is, for example, if she were to suddenly smile sweetly at her sister, insisting that the untidy state of the bedroom didn't bother her at all, Lynette would immediately become suspicious.

By the same token, if Lynette's room became miraculously spick and span, we would know that Audrey was perfectly justified in looking for an ulterior motive.

Interacting with people and objects

Fictional characters must interact with the people and things around them as realistically as possible. If they bang a knee on a table leg, they will cry 'ouch!', if you given them a gift, they will say 'thank you', and if you trick them out of their life savings, they will want to have their revenge.

Action, reaction and interaction are central to any work of fiction and vital to the twist in the tale.

CHECKLIST

1. Will your opening line grab the reader's attention?

2. Have you combined the dialogue and action without relying on words like 'he/she said'?

3. Do you understand the meaning of every word you have used?

4. Have you kept the story moving from start to finish?

5.   Do your characters react realistically to one another and their surroundings?

ASSIGNMENT

Imagine a couple in a car. Using a combination of dialogue and action, write a conversation between the woman driver and her male, backseat driving companion. Their relationship to one another is up to you but in order to achieve maximum realism and reader identification, if you are male, you **must** write it from the **man's** viewpoint and if you are female, from the **woman's**.

4
A Twisted Mind Helps

BEGINNING WITH THE ENDING

One of the commonest mistakes novice writers make when they attempt to write fiction is to begin writing aimlessly, with no idea where the storyline is going to take them. This approach may sound wonderfully artistic and creative but it invariably results in a rambling tale, full of stops, starts and viewpoint changes.

Writing backwards
The most effective way to approach a twist in the tale is to think of an ending then work out how you are going to achieve it. To all intents and purposes, therefore, the skilled twist author writes backwards.

Creating identifiable characters
The skill of the short story writer lies in developing identifiable characters who interact realistically with one another and their surroundings. Under these circumstances, the author can effectively interpret the interplay, provide suitably atmospheric settings and oversee events to their logical conclusion.

Changing the outcome
This is not to say that the storyline cannot change. In a straightforward three-handed romance, for example, the reader will expect the girl to choose the right boy from two very different suitors.

The writer's initial intention may be for her to choose the solid, reliable one but as the story progresses in its non-twist format, the circumstances could alter, as illustrated in Fig. 3.

Possible outcomes depending on Jill's character

1. Jill decides to stay with Bob. He will always be there for her and

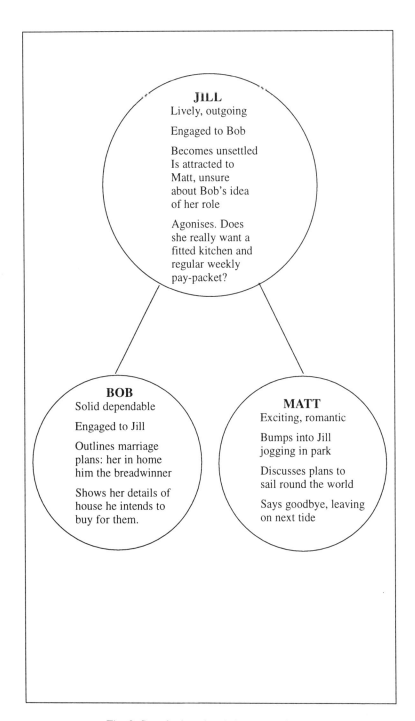

JILL
Lively, outgoing

Engaged to Bob

Becomes unsettled
Is attracted to
Matt, unsure
about Bob's idea
of her role

Agonises. Does
she really want a
fitted kitchen and
regular weekly
pay-packet?

BOB
Solid dependable

Engaged to Jill

Outlines marriage
plans: her in home
him the breadwinner

Shows her details of
house he intends to
buy for them.

MATT
Exciting, romantic

Bumps into Jill
jogging in park

Discusses plans to
sail round the world

Says goodbye, leaving
on next tide

Fig. 3. Sample three-handed romance format.

whilst Matt's lifestyle sounds exciting, she could never be sure of his commitment to her.

2. Jill runs off with Matt. She cannot stay with Bob if he is going to make major decisions like where they will live without consulting her.

The choice Jill makes will depend on how her personality evolves as the story progresses but a twist tale has a far more complicated structure.

There is no leeway in a twist story to allow the characters to take off in a direction of their own. We need to know right at the start who will end up with whom and why.

Constructing a twist

In the twisted version of our three-handed romance, the writer might be working towards an ending in which Jill is left high and dry while the two men sail off happily together into the sunset.

Once we know the outcome, we can direct our characters to set the traps and then spring them for us in all the right places. We will be looking at methods of setting those traps, or 'signposting', later in the book. First, we must think about the storyline and then ask ourselves that vital question, 'What if . . .?'

TWISTING THE 'WHAT IF?' FACTOR

Ask any writer how they come up with their plots and they will probably tell you that they think of either a character or a situation and then ask themselves the question 'what if . . .?'

The same technique is true of the twist in the tale but for our purposes, the 'what if?' factor must have a slight kink in it.

Sample twist storyline

A young woman is waiting for her long-term boyfriend in the lobby of a large office block. *What if* he fails to turn up? There are a number of options:

● He's stood her up.
● He's had an accident.
● He forgot that he would be working late.

Any one of these examples would work as a romantic story but the twist writer will be looking for an angle and this is where you will find a somewhat cynical or twisted outlook invaluable.

The cynical approach

Sifting through the above options, I find myself most attracted to the second one, where the poor chap has a, possibly fatal, accident.

The heroine has been waiting for some time. Her colleagues are leaving and soon the steady stream of office workers thins to a trickle. A security guard notices her anxiously consulting her watch. He strikes up a conversation with her and she tells him all about her relationship. She hints that her boyfriend can be quite cruel but in spite of his shortcomings, she loves him. He's very late and she's sure something must have happened to him.

They discuss the possibility that she might have been mistaken about the time and place but she assures him that her boyfriend confirmed the arrangements by phone only a few hours before.

The girl becomes more distraught until, in an effort to set her mind at rest, the security guard offers to telephone first their flat and then her boyfriend's office. With no reply from either, he discreetly telephones the local hospital. Yes, he is told, there has been an accident, a fatal one.

It is at this point that the cynical twist writer reveals the true question which is not '**what if he fails to turn up?**' but '**what if the heroine knew he wasn't going to turn up all along?**'

Setting the trap

She has, of course, set up the accident and the wait in the office lobby is her alibi. The security guard will confirm her distressed state. Fellow employees from the insurance company where she works saw her waiting. And when she collects on the policy she recently took out on her boyfriend's life, her colleagues will be relieved that she has something to cushion the blow of her loss.

PLOTTING AND PLANNING

Twist stories can be quite complex but this does not mean that they are heavily plotted. Once again, the small number of words counts against the twist writer.

Keeping it simple

With a limited number of characters, a limited timescale and, in some cases, as few as 500 words, any attempt to work out a complicated plotline, full of red herrings and suspicious characters, is going to end in awful failure.

We have already noted that a short story is an incident and in the case of a magazine twist in the tale, the intricacies of the plot must be dealt with as briefly as possible.

However, providing you avoid deviating too far from the basic plot-line, it is possible to introduce a note of flexibility. For example, the basic plot for our young lady and her accident-prone boyfriend was relatively simple but *what if* it turns out to be a case of mistaken identity and it wasn't him who was killed at all?

Or perhaps he was killed but not in the way our heroine planned and she is unable to collect on the policy.

You may come up with a number of variations but the basic plotline must not change, i.e. **A girl is waiting for a man who she knows is not going to arrive**.

As the characters begin to develop, so you can plan the course of events. It is at this stage that you will be able to make your decision about the final twist but be sure you have it firmly fixed in your mind before you attempt to finish the story.

FRAMING THE VICTIM

The central character in a twist story may well be the perpetrator of a particularly unpleasant crime. One of the problems a twist writer has to solve, therefore, is how to let the protagonist commit the crime and get away with it without upsetting the reader's moral sensibilities.

Sympathising with the murderer

In the plot outlined above, our heroine hinted to the security guard that her boyfriend had a cruel streak. Maybe he thinks nothing of giving her a good beating, plays around with other women or is obsessively jealous.

By the time we've finished with him, the reader will be as desperate as our heroine is to get rid of him and get their own back on him for his appalling behaviour.

Rebounding on the murderer

However, in this particular story, our central character could turn out to be the victim of her own vicious scheme. This time, the hatchet job must be applied to her character.

Maybe she is lying about her boyfriend. He's weak and was easily tricked into making her the beneficiary of his insurance policy. When she is unable to collect on it, we are relieved that she hasn't got away with her plan.

MISLEADING ISN'T CHEATING

The art of twist story writing is to give the reader as much information as possible but framed in such a way that nothing is exactly what it appears to be. This effect is achieved by the use of ambiguous words and phrases which are deliberately designed to mislead the reader.

Concealing the truth

The following extract is taken from a story I wrote entitled 'Face to Face'. The central characters are Toby and Jane, a married couple who appear to be interior decorators. The setting is a luxury flat they had hoped to purchase but couldn't afford. The couple have, apparently, been engaged by the new owners to advise on the renovations and decor:

> *The sound of the front door crashing open broke into their conversation and Toby flew to the landing outside the flat.*
>
> *'It's all right,' he reassured Jane as she reached his side, 'It's only the carpenter. He's stacking the new floorboards in the hall downstairs.' He let out a low, soft whistle, 'Just look at it all, I wouldn't like to have to lug that lot up these stairs.'*
>
> *'You'd better watch out then,' Jane giggled, 'If he catches sight of you, he might try to rope you in to give him a hand.'*
>
> (Adèle Ramet, *Bella* 1993)

It all sounds perfectly normal but there's something not quite right. Toby should be directing operations, not skulking about upstairs. In his line of work, he should know how many floorboards the carpenter will need.

Sprinkling clues

A couple of paragraphs on, Jane mentions how pleased she is that the new floor is going to be laid. 'That gaping hole,' she says, 'really gives me the creeps.' Toby, however, is quick to reassure her. 'It can't hurt you,' he tells her. A truth which becomes clear when it is finally revealed that the couple are, in fact, ghosts, who met their death by crashing through rotten floorboards when they were viewing the property.

They fully intend to stay in their dream home, using their spiritual powers to influence the new owners into decorating the flat in exactly the way they want it.

Revealing the truth

Far from concealing their true state, clues or 'signposts' have been liberally sprinkled throughout the story. The characters never actually touch anything, they 'work their way around the room' and when they heard the carpenter arrive, Toby 'flew' to the landing.

The story's final twist also explains why Jane 'giggled' at the thought of the carpenter catching sight of Toby and it is these dropped hints and subtle clues that achieve reader satisfaction in a twist in the tale. Without them, the story has no substance and would be a disappointing cheat.

CASE STUDIES

Jill loses direction

Jill is a teacher in her early thirties, whose love of reading gives her the inspiration for unlimited original stories.

Her opening lines are perfect, pulling you straight into the action and there is lots of vibrant dialogue between the characters, but half-way through, her stories lose impetus because she can never decide on the ending.

She always hopes that, once she has begun to write, the characters will interact sufficiently with one another to indicate a suitable twist but without a clear ending to aim for, Jill loses direction and is never able to construct a viable plot.

Barbara twists the tale

Barbara is a lively, enthusiastic divorcee. Despite a very unhappy marriage, she has a well-developed, wry sense of humour which she puts to excellent use in her twist stories.

Her past experience has taught her that it can be very useful to expect the unexpected so she is able to think up suitably devious endings as soon as her characters are formed in her mind. Only when she has decided on the ending does she work on the interaction between her characters to bring realism to the story.

CHECKLIST

1. Do you know how your story is going to end?

2. Is the 'what if' question sufficiently twisted?

3. Is the plot too complicated?

4. Have you planned your story from start to finish?

5. Are you sure you have not cheated?

ASSIGNMENT

The following sentences are open to two different interpretations. I have set out the most obvious one, your task is to find the hidden meaning (answers on p. 116).

Example: *Puffing and panting as he climbed higher and higher, he wondered if he would ever reach the top.*
(a) A man struggling up a mountain
(b) A small child climbing a flight of stairs

1. The sea of faces waited expectantly for him to deliver his speech.
(a) A tutor delivering a lecture
(b) ....

2. *Deftly, she fastened off the row of neat stitches.*
(a) A seamstress finishing off a garment
(b) ....

3. *She hated never being allowed to go anywhere by herself.*
(a) A young girl
(b) ....

4. *Heads turned as he posed and strutted in time to the throbbing music.*
(a) A John Travolta look-alike in a disco
(b) ....

5
Signposting

TAKING YOUR READER ALONG THE SCENIC ROUTE

As we saw in the previous chapter, in a twist story, it is essential that you do not cheat by concealing a vital piece of information and then revealing it at the end of the story. All this will do is to leave you with an unconvincing ending and a very disappointed reader.

Misdirecting the reader

In order to achieve an acceptable twist in the tale, you need to plant signposts which will effectively misdirect the reader along a number of side turnings before leading them finally to your intended destination.

To help clarify this technique, think of writing straightforward romantic stories as travelling down a motorway, whilst twist stories take the scenic route.

With a romance, your route from beginning to end is mapped out but what, at first sight, appears to be a clear road inevitably becomes strewn with obstacles. Traffic jams, diversions, unexpected incidents litter the highway but the couple steadfastly remain on the path to happiness, emerging relatively unscathed from their journey to spend the rest of their days firmly united.

Sidetracking

In a twist story, the writer deliberately avoids the motorway in favour of the country lanes. In this way, the reader becomes sidetracked by a variety of picturesque sights and sounds.

We may potter along an old farmtrack or rest awhile at a riverside pub. The reader is never quite sure where we are going or even why we are going there but whichever route we take, it is imperative that the sidetracks inevitably lead us back to where we ought to be.

PLANTING THE CLUES

We have looked briefly at some of the methods of using misleading signposts in the previous chapter and the technique of planting clues to convey information and move the story forward is found in all forms of fiction writing. There are a number of ways you can do this:

- through dialogue
- through description
- through action
- through flashback.

Using dialogue

As we saw in Chapter 3, dialogue fulfils a number of functions in fiction and will reveal a great deal of useful information. In the story 'Face to Face', Jane is saddened by the fact that the couple who have purchased 'their' flat are unlikely to have children. She tells Toby:

> *'Somehow, I can't ever see children featuring in their lifestyle.'*
> *'Definitely not. But then,' Toby's voice was gruff, 'Things don't always work out the way we plan them, do they?'*

At this stage in the story, we are still unaware that they are ghosts and this short piece of dialogue appears to refer to the fact they were unable to buy the family home they wanted. With hindsight, however, we can see that it refers to their untimely death before they had a chance to start a family of their own.

Using description and action

The combination of description and action can be very effective in planting clues. From the following narrative, it would appear that E. Evans' story entitled 'Led Astray' (*Bella* 1995) is centred around a troublesome toddler:

> *Josh closed his lips and turned his head away. He didn't want strained beef. He wanted chocolate pudding. He sensed she was in a hurry. Perhaps Chris was coming round. The thought of Chris made him pout. This gave her the chance to tip a spoonful of mush into his mouth. Spluttering, he spat it into his bib.*

As the story progresses, it quickly becomes clear that all is far from well in this particular household. Through a fast-moving combination of dialogue, description and action, the reader is misled into believing that the story is about a young mother whose husband has been given an early release from a long prison sentence.

A conversation between the hated Chris and the woman, Sal, as she spoonfeeds Josh reveals a more worrying scenario:

> *Chris gripped her hands, 'We knew we had to face it sometime. Luke's got to know,' Josh caught the nod in his direction, 'You can't hide him, can you? In fact, I'm surprised nobody's tipped Luke off.'*

By now, the reader is thoroughly convinced. During Luke's time in prison, Sal and Chris have had an affair and baby Josh is the result.

Using flashback

It is at this point that E. Evans introduces flashback to further heighten the tension:

> *'Oh, Chris, I wish we'd gone away before he came back.'*
> *'I wanted to. You're the one who wanted to stop here.'*
> *'I couldn't let him come back to an empty house.'*
> *'That's always been your trouble, Sal. You're too loyal. You should have got out years ago, instead of staying with a husband who knocked you about.'*

Firmly hooked now, we read on to discover that Luke is a hardened criminal with a history of violence. In a vain attempt to delay the inevitable, Sal and Chris bundle Josh into his coat but just as they are wheeling him out of the kitchen, Luke arrives. They hurriedly push Josh into the lounge and shut the door but to no avail. Bored and irritable, Josh squeals and screams until he is discovered by the menacingly powerful Luke.

It is here that E. Evans once again uses flashback to reveal the very clever twist and bring the story to a highly satisfactory end.

Josh is not, in fact, a toddler at all but Sal's husband and Luke's father. Shortly after 'shopping' his own son to the police, he was involved in a car accident which left him in this appallingly brain-damaged state.

As if this were not enough, the author includes a final horrific twist as she reveals in the story's closing paragraph below that the car crash in which Josh received his injuries was no accident but had been set up by an embittered, vengeful, Luke:

Josh eyed the large man as he bent over him. He sensed he didn't like him.

'Well, well, Dad,' Luke murmured, 'Who'd have thought that brake would last for a whole year. I couldn't have frayed it enough when I was out on bail. Still, all's well that ends well, eh? That'll teach you to try to do me out of my cut from the post office job by setting me up with the police.'

(E. Evans, *Bella* 1995)

FORETELLING THE FUTURE WITH FLASHBACK

Whilst flashback is an effective method of revealing background information, it also serves to move the story forward by indicating that whatever is about to take place has happened at least once before. For example:

He stood, glaring furiously at the damaged bumper. If he'd told her once, he'd told her a thousand times not to use his car. Only last week, he'd warned her that if she so much as glanced in its direction, their relationship would be over for good.

From this short flashback we know that they argued about the car last week, that he'd given her a clear warning how he would react if she disobeyed him and that a confrontation between the couple is now inevitable.

Blending flashback with action

Flashbacks should blend smoothly into the text through short snatches of dialogue, action and description. Avoid long passages, which can make you forget where you are in a story, and never jerk back without warning.

Flashback must be:

- integral to the action
- relevant to the story
- emotionally linked with the present.

Used correctly it can be one of the most effective ways of providing both genuine and misleading information, as well as moving the story forward at a very fast pace.

TURNING AND TWISTING

A tale with a good single twist is very desirable and perfectly saleable. A double twist, one in which the reader is given two surprises, is even better so it is worth taking a close look at your original storyline to see if it can be improved upon.

However, most sought after of all is the triple twist which is not only the most difficult to write but also the most saleable format.

Twisting once, twice, three times

For the single twist, we know that we need the following elements:

- strong characterisation
- realistic dialogue
- action, reaction and interaction
- imaginative signposting
- originality (this will be covered in the next chapter).

Using the plot in Chapter 4 about the young woman waiting for her boyfriend, the basic storyline offers only a single twist but by continuing to twist and turn, it is possible to introduce a double and even a triple twist, as shown in Fig. 4.

Why not twist again?

In theory, there is no reason why a fourth twist could not be added to this storyline.

The confirmation of the boyfriend's death could be due to a case of mistaken identity on the part of the hospital. The story's final twist could then have the boyfriend returning home to discover his late girlfriend's body. A fitting end, if only there were enough room for it on the page.

Running out of words

It is a skilful writer indeed who could manage more than three twists within the confines of a one-page slot and still find room for characterisation and background information.

The discipline of writing stories for women's magazines is a strict one, offering little freedom to wander away from the initial plot. A fourth twist is near impossible to achieve effectively in 850–1,200 words.

Single Twist

1	2	3	4
Girl waits, apparently anxiously, for boyfriend	She knows he will not arrive because she has arranged for him to meet with an accident	Her plan succeeds, he dies	Insurance company pays out

Double Twist

1	2	3	4
Girl waits for boy	She knows he will not arrive	Her plan succeeds, he dies	Query on insurance
5	**6**	**7**	**8**
There is a hitch	He is dead but not from the cause she planned	Suicide is suspected and payment witheld	She cannot prove other-wise without implicating herself

Triple Twist

1	2	3	4
Girl waits for boy	She knows he will not arrive	Her plan succeeds, he dies	Query on insurance
5	**6**	**7**	**8**
There is a hitch	He is dead but not from the cause she planned	Suicide is suspected and payment witheld	She cannot prove other-wise without implicating herself
9	**10**	**11**	**12**
She goes home	She blames boyfriend for the failure of her plan	In her temper she accidentally springs her own trap	She dies

Fig. 4. Stages from single to double to triple twist.

SEXUAL STEREOTYPING

Despite the current emphasis on political correctness and equal opportunities within the workplace, we still have a tendency to equate certain professions with one or other sex. For a quick association test, glance briefly at the list below and write down the first sex ('male' or 'female') that comes into your head:

Nurse ....

Secretary ....

Barrister ....

Professor ....

Electrician ....

Plumber ....

Receptionist ....

Engineer ....

Psychiatrist ....

Surgeon ....

Scientist ....

Model ....

Any one of the above occupations can be and is undertaken by both men and women but you will probably have put 'female' for nurse despite the fact that there are a growing number of male nurses and midwives. So much so, in fact, that the title 'Matron' was dropped some years ago in favour of 'Senior Nursing Officer'.

Secretary is another title which is invariably associated with women. Although there are male secretaries performing general office duties, they are few and far between. However, the title itself can be applied to a number of other jobs. For example, a company secretary, Parliamentary private secretary, club secretary, etc.

In real life, female professors, surgeons and scientists are as commonplace as male models, but in fiction, more often than not on a first reading, our initial reaction is to sexually stereotype the first three characters as men and the fourth as a woman.

Relying on a preconceived image

The skilled twist writer will seize on any and every such opportunity for immediate sexual stereotyping, knowing that overturning a fixed image in the reader's mind will make for a much more effective final twist.

Set out below are just a few examples of themes which benefit from the use of sexual stereotyping:

- A wedding service conducted by a minister who turns out to be the bride's mother.

- A psychiatrist treating her husband's mistress.

- A husband calming his suspicious wife's fears about his relationship with a colleague 'Professor' Smith.

- A barrister winning the confidence of a male chauvinist client.

Are they who they appear to be?

The effect you are always aiming for is to make the reader believe a character is someone or something they are not. Careful signposting and informative flashbacks will create the impression that all is not quite what it seems but the reader shouldn't be able to put his or her finger on exactly what is wrong until it is time to reveal the final twist.

CASE STUDIES

James goes for a surprise ending

James left school at eighteen to take a job as a computer programmer. Now in his early twenties, he is keen to develop his writing skills and ultimately see his stories in print.

A keen fan of horror and fantasy fiction, he has a vivid imagination but tends to save up all the vital information in order to spring it on the reader in the last paragraph in the form of a surprise ending. Unfortunately, this only leaves the reader feeling cheated and the twist invariably falls flat.

Roger finds sexual stereotyping advantageous

Roger is a human resources manager in his late forties who is very sensitive to sexist attitudes within the workplace. Knowing that the title 'nurse' is associated with women and that the term 'twin' implies siblings of the same sex, he has the idea for a story about an unscrupulous male nurse with an equally unpleasant twin sister.

This clever use of sexual stereotyping misleads the reader into believing that the nursing twin is female when he is, in fact, male, resulting in a highly effective twist in the tale.

CHECKLIST

1. Can the signposts be interpreted in at least two ways?

2. Are the clues fair?

3. Are the flashbacks short and relevant?

4. Is the final twist realistic?

5. Can it be extended to a double or a triple twist?

ASSIGNMENT

Write a scene in which a wife is trying to conceal a murder weapon immediately after killing her husband. Convey, through the use of flashback, why she killed him.

6
Finding Original Ideas

It has been said that there are only seven storylines in the world. If this is true then it would appear to be impossible to come up with an original idea.

Originality is, however, the one element that editors will always seize upon, so how do you achieve it?

LOOKING FOR THE ANGLE

There may not be many standard plots but there are an infinite number of angles. Even the most well-used storyline can prove successful providing it is approached from an unusual point of view.

Train yourself to consider every possible aspect of a situation or relationship. Remember that in a twist story things are never quite what they seem. Using this fact as a basis from which to begin, it is possible to bring a fresh slant to almost any plot.

Remember, too, that whilst an original storyline is something every editor looks for and every writer strives to achieve, there is one advantage to tried and tested plots – you know they are going to work.

DRAWING INSPIRATION FROM THE SPIRIT WORLD

Ghosts are a great comfort to the twist writer. They provide an infinite variety of plots and serve to enhance the story in a number of ways.

Ghostly functions:

- being the central character

- being the central character's adversary

- becoming the object of the central character's affections

- being the instrument through which the central character turns the tables

- sending spirit messages

- providing the final twist.

Haunting themes

Stories with a ghostly theme contain, by their very definition, an element of suspense and as such are ideal for the twist in the tale. Events which would be inexplicable in any other sense suddenly become perfectly clear when attributed to influences from the spirit world.

Twist ghosts are usually fairly modern so there is no need to resort to detailed historical backgrounds. Like their earthbound counterparts, they are invariably streetwise and may well be endowed with a wicked sense of humour. Ghostly tales for the women's magazine market tend to be light and amusing rather than dark and sinister.

Spiritualism and mediums

One of the most popular methods of introducing a spirit into a tale is through a medium. This storyline offers a variety of plots and the fiction writer can allow his or her imagination to run riot on the characterisation.

Mediums can and do range from eccentric elderly ladies clad in shabby crocheted shawls to hard-headed charlatans who choose their crystal-gazing costumes with impeccable care.

Spirit guides are equally colourful, from the classic Red Indian Chief to frighteningly solemn children, and once again, an injection of humour is invariably included in order to lighten the tone.

TWISTING WITH LITTLE OLD LADIES

One misconception with regard to twist stories is that they invariably feature a stereotyped little old lady. Everyman's image of a granny, apple-cheeked, grey hair in a bun, she somehow miraculously over-powers a young, athletic male assailant until, by the end of the story, he is screaming for mercy.

However, in common with some of the other twist techniques we have looked at, this scenario is open to misinterpretation.

Taking account of past experience

The key to the 'old lady' story is understanding that, just because someone has passed the age of retirement, it doesn't mean they've lost all their knowledge, skills and personality.

What did she do before?

Depending on your character's age and education, she could have been any one of the following before feminism became fashionable and society accepted that women were capable of being something other than wives and mothers:

- a nuclear physicist
- a research scientist
- an army driver
- a mail plane pilot
- a member of the Secret Service
- a knife-thrower's/conjurer's assistant
- a contortionist/professional gymnast.

Providing you plant the clues about a past career in the right places within the story and your characterisation is strong enough, there is no limit to the skills with which you can endow your 'little old ladies'.

Grannies aren't necessarily old

It is worth bearing in mind, too, that the granny of today could easily be under forty and your characterisation must take account of this. One useful exercise you might like to try with a group of fellow writers is a rapid-fire brainstorming game.

Write the word 'Grandmother' on a board or large sheet of paper and ask the following questions in quick succession:

1. How old is she?

2. What colour is her hair?

3. What colour are her eyes?

4. How tall is she?

5. What's her figure like?

6. What is she wearing?

7.   Does she have a job?

8.   What are her hobbies?

9.   Does she wear make-up?

10. What is she doing right at this moment?

The description built up in this way often varies considerably from the elderly stereotype.

The granny of the 1990s may well be pictured wearing brightly coloured shell suits and trainers. Her hair is often dyed, she likes chunky jewellery, her make-up is skilfully applied and she combines a hectic job with running a home, offering support to her adult children and attending keep fit and aerobics classes.

If she does own a rocking chair, she probably bought it at a boot sale and devotes any spare time she may have to stripping it down, renovating and restoring it to pristine condition.

DISPOSING OF CLEVER CATS AND DIMWITTED DOGS

We'll be looking at over-used plots in more detail later in this chapter but one evergreen favourite ploy is to have the murder unwittingly committed by the family pet.

You can't kill an animal

When the pet is the sole recipient of a spouse's love and attention or worse still, the sole beneficiary of a wealthy relative's will, the plot possibilities are plain to see.

However, if you do decide to feature an animal in your story, particularly a furry one with four legs and a tail, make sure it emerges unscathed. Failure to do so will almost certainly result in rejection as your editor will know that harming an animal results in a postbag bulging with letters of complaint. In contrast, a murdered child will rarely provoke any reaction at all.

Remember that twist story animals are inclined to be formidable adversaries and in any confrontation, the human character is likely to come off a great deal worse than his or her intended victim.

MURDERING YOUR SPOUSE

For some inexplicable reason, this storyline is also incredibly popular with twist story writers. There is no doubt that fiction writing can be a tension-relieving exercise and murdering a long-term partner on paper can prove a trouble-free and quite satisfactory alternative to the illegal and somewhat messier real thing.

Murdering your husband

This is possibly the easiest option as the majority of women's magazine readers are female. Once again, the key to using these storylines is characterisation and most women will identify with the wife whose husband has become an intolerable irritant.

Humour is also a helpful ingredient in this type of twist. Murder is a serious crime so it helps to include an element of black comedy in order to make it acceptable to the reader.

Avoiding true life realism

A story featuring a battered wife who is driven to murder her husband is worth trying, providing it is very sensitively written, but such gritty realism may be difficult to place within the women's magazine market.

For the most part, the successful murdering wife usually, although not always, gets her come-uppance.

Murdering your wife

Successfully murdering your wife is a little more complicated than killing your husband.

In order to appeal to your mainly female readership, the hard-done-by husband must be particularly badly henpecked or be heading for an especially nasty fate at his wife's hands before you let him loose with a murder weapon.

Choosing your weapon

There are two ways to kill someone in a twist story:

1. On purpose

2. By accident

Because the stories are so short, slow-acting poisons or intricate booby traps are out of the question. It is, therefore, necessary to find a quick, easy way to dispose of the victim.

Listed below are some of the methods most favoured by twist authors:

● stabbing

● sabotaging the car

● pushing – over a cliff, down the stairs, on a slippery surface, etc.

● drowning

● locking in the cellar of an unoccupied house

● dropping an electrical appliance into the bath.

Causing a chain reaction

Whether the murder is accidental or deliberate, it is helpful if the method turns out to be a metaphorical double-edged sword.

Your story can be enhanced if the actual murder process sets off a chain reaction which places the murderer in some kind of perilous situation.

For example, in her story 'Family Fortunes', Joyce Begg uses a brilliant variation on the 'dropping an electrical appliance into the bath' theme.

For years, Frank has been trying to persuade his Aunt Grace to sell her valuable but run-down house to no avail. When, once again, she refuses, a murder weapon conveniently comes to hand in the shape of a faulty bathroom heater which she begs him to mend. At first, Frank insists he is too busy but then it dawns on him that he can turn the situation to his advantage and Aunt Grace is delighted when he arrives, complete with toolbox, the following day:

The heater still looked dangerous. There was a cord which hung down over the bath, so whoever was in it only had to reach up and pull. One decent tug would have the heater in the water, resulting in electrocution.

Frank planned to straighten it and reattach it to the wall so it would look secure, even if it wasn't. It must switch on easily and come off the wall easily all at the same time.

He craned his neck to examine it. Then he looked round for a decent foothold, to see the thing at closer quarters.

The chair that usually stood by the bath was missing so, holding on to the ancient pipes, he levered himself up on to the rim of the bath, placing his feet carefully and twisting towards the heater.

He never knew what happened next. With a shout of alarm, he lost his footing and crashed into the bath, striking his head on the cast-iron edge.

At this point, it is revealed that, despite her innocent demeanour, Aunt Grace had murderous plans of her own:

Downstairs, Grace heard the crash and the sudden silence. Slowly making her way upstairs, she called and got no answer.

Frank lay in the bath in a heap, his neck at a most unlikely angle. She felt for a pulse. There was none.

Then she fetched the washcloth and scrubbed at the edge of the bath and at the soles of Frank's shoes until every trace of cooking oil was removed.

It was a tragedy, everyone said. So young, so successful and such a help to his aunt.

Grace played the part of the distracted relative whenever she had an audience but as soon as she was on her own, she started on the list of renovations that would restore the house to what it once was.

Frank's company was a valuable asset and its sale would bring in a lot of money. Frank had never made a will. Helen was not his wife so Grace was his sole heir – just as he had been hers.

('Family Fortunes', Joyce Begg, *Bella* 1995)

Using the device of role reversal, combined with some clever characterisation and planning, Joyce effectively gives the storyline a highly original slant.

PUTTING THE MALE VIEWPOINT IN A WOMAN'S WORLD

Until the arrival of the twist in the tale, the majority of stories for women's magazines were romances written by female writers.

However, because the twist tale encompasses such a wide range of genres, it offers an excellent opportunity for men to break into today's women's magazine fiction market.

Understanding women's interests

Providing they bear in mind that they are writing for a predominantly female readership, male writers can and do bring a refreshing slant to the style and feel of the stories.

In his story 'Breaking Even', Fred Clayson's central character offers a positive male image to the readership of *Bella*.

Bob Harris is a loving, hard-working husband whose business has been badly hit by the recession. He needs to take drastic action if he is to survive and in the following extract, it appears he has been driven to crime:

> *By the light of the moon, he stood scrutinising the dazzling goods in the jeweller's window. It would be so easy.*
>
> *He took a deep breath and stepped up to the plate glass. His hand seemed to be separate from his body and he watched, fascinated, as he threw a brick through the window. He felt like a spectator, watching the action in slow motion.*

It is clear from his actions that Bob takes no pride in what he has done and is terrified by the subsequent screech of the shop's alarm. Later, when it is revealed that he is not a thief but a glass merchant using a somewhat unorthodox method to drum up business, we can only feel pleased that his plan has succeeded.

Turning to crime

Many of the tales written by men are crime stories dealing with burglary, fraud, computer crime and car theft. They may also be centred around the down-trodden male in the workplace, fighting off challenges to his authority by younger, more dynamic or overbearing colleagues.

PLOTS TO AVOID

Many of the more familiar plots have already been mentioned in this chapter. Murdering your spouse in particular, although popular, is a very well-worn theme and there are several others which should be avoided.

Over-used twist plots

- Nephew dies attempting to murder rich aunt's animal beneficiary.

- Pet dog accidentally shuts owner's jealous spouse in cellar of deserted house.

- Victim poisoned and buried in the garden where, months later, discoloured plants grow to reveal body.

- As above but victim had time to leave message in the form of seeds sown in the pattern of the murder's initials.

- Hospital story where the character we think is the patient turns out to be the doctor.

- Murderer sabotages brakes on the victim's car then forgets and drives the car away.

- Fake fortune-tellers and mediums suddenly discovering that they really do have 'second sight'.

The editorial guidelines from *Take A Break* add even more overworked plots to this list:

- The heroine/narrator is revealed to be a cat, dog, fox, car, etc.

- The policeman/woman is really a singing telegram.

- A character's mysterious arrangements turn out to be for a surprise party.

- The woman discovers her husband's secret lover is a man (or vice versa).

- The murder victim ends up on a compost heap.

- The perpetrator's murder plan backfires and s/he eats the poison.

- Anything to do with poisonous mushrooms or tampering with car brakes.

- A shifty antiques dealer dupes an old lady out of what he thinks is a priceless antique and it turns out she is making them by the dozen.

- Anything to do with twins.

- Someone nervous about a first day at school turns out to be the teacher or about a wedding – the vicar, or an interview – the interviewer.

'And then I woke up'

However, perhaps the most overworked storyline of all has to be the 'dream' story where the strange events are explained by the central character waking to reveal 'it had all been a dream'. This well-worn chestnut is considered to be the cheat ending to end all cheat endings and should be avoided at all costs.

Injecting originality into the storyline

With the exception of the 'dream' story, it is sometimes possible to rework a tried and tested theme.

Whilst the twist will need to be especially original, well-drawn characters and plenty of realistic interaction can serve to counteract the familiarity of a well-used plot.

People read about people and providing it is approached from a fresh slant, there is an element of fun involved for both the writer and the reader in turning a storyline on its head and coming up with a really original angle.

WHERE DO YOU GET YOUR IDEAS?

Whilst it is possible to use a familiar plot successfully, it is obviously far better to come up with a completely original idea.

Every writer has their own method of finding ideas and for the most part, they draw on their own experiences and surroundings for inspiration. The twist story writer has a particularly cynical view of life and this, in itself, offers all kinds of opportunities.

Drawing on your own experience

Twist writer Fred Clayson believes firmly that 'a devious mind is a prerequisite for any short story writer'.

He finds reading through a dictionary or encyclopaedia helpful, simply 'soaking up the various words and headings'. A single word in a newspaper or, as on one occasion, a box of matches, can trigger off inspiration.

Seeing story potential

Anything and everything around you has story potential. Two colleagues at work chatting by a drinks vending machine might, for example, simply be discussing the weather. However, a chance remark that the payroll computer is affected by sudden changes in humidity and you have the beginnings of a twist story.

One payroll clerk in financial difficulties combined with a cup of liquid which will create the appropriate atmospheric conditions will provide you with the basic ingredients for a twist plot.

Breeding grounds for ideas

- The home
- The workplace
- Shops
- Bus queues and on buses
- Train stations and on trains
- Ferry ports and on ferries
- Airports and on planes
- Social and sports clubs
- Parties
- School gates
- Nurseries
- Playgrounds
- Factual television and radio programmes
- Articles within your chosen magazine
- Newspapers

As soon as you alight upon a suitable situation, always ask yourself 'what if?'

CHECKLIST

1. Do you understand the motivation of your characters?

2. Are they behaving realistically within their given situation?

3. Is the plot believable?

4. Do you have an original twist?

5. Have you asked the question 'what if?'?

ASSIGNMENT

An elderly widow wakes in her chair to find a burglar stealing her things. He is obviously nervous and she begins to talk to him, calms him

down and when he is offguard, overpowers him and is ab
police. What did she do and how was she able to do it? Use
below as a guide:

1. Approximately how old is she?

2. What does she look like?

3. Was she married and if so, what did her husband do?

4. What sort of childhood did she have?

5. Did she go out to work and if so, what did she do?

6. Does she have any unusual talents or skills?

7. Did she bring up a family?

8. Do any family members live nearby?

9. Was she in any of the armed forces?

10. Does she overcome him by luck or judgement?

7
Identifying with the Reader

UNDERSTANDING WHICH STORY YOU ARE REALLY WRITING

A good twist in the tale is not unlike a magician's illusion. Working on the principle that seeing is believing, the illusionist makes use of the fact that the eye can be very deceptive.

By keeping the audience transfixed on the events onstage, the mechanics of the illusion are concealed from view in such a way that only a trained onlooker will be able to detect how the trick is done.

Using diversionary tactics

The most effective illusionists are those who build up the tension through a combination of theatrical costume, clever lighting and dramatic sets.

Common sense tells us that it's just a trick. However, the scene being played out onstage transfixes the audience into believing that the impossible is happening before their eyes.

Using the same concept, albeit in a less dramatic form, the main theme in a twist story is an illusion. Something else is always going on behind the scenes.

The best way to understand how this technique is achieved is to use a basic twist storyline.

Creating the illusion

Jeff and Liz are in a café discussing Jeff's forthcoming marriage. Liz appears hurt and angry. The impression given is that Jeff is Liz's son and she is trying to stop him leaving home. However, the twist in the tale is that Jeff is not Liz's son but her widowed father.

Whose story are you telling

For this scenario it is important that the vocabulary is chosen with care in order to imply that Jeff is much younger than he actually is, whilst Liz must seem a lot older. The ensuing conversation must, however, be equally applicable to a daughter and son as to a father and daughter:

> *'I don't understand why you're in such a hurry to get married,'* Liz *tried to keep the note of desperation out of her voice, 'Anyone would think you had to . . .' her voice tailed off as she felt the hairs prickle on the back of her neck.*
>
> *Jeff's blue eyes burned with fury, 'What's wrong with you?' he clenched his fist until the knuckles showed white, 'You just can't accept that I've fallen in love can you? Well it's time you realised that if you don't like it,' he paused, choosing his words with care, 'It'd be better for both of us if you stayed out of my life from now on.'*

During the conversation, it is imperative that you avoid any reference to parents or children.

Avoiding the truth

The desired effect is achieved not so much by what you put in as by what you leave out.

In order to provide an effective twist, the writer needs to identify clearly with a teenage boy as these will be the emotions, arguments and logic you will be conveying. It is only when the twist is revealed, that it will become obvious that the same emotions and reactions are equally valid in relation to a single parent.

WRITING FOR A SPECIFIC READERSHIP

Reader identification and empathy with the reader is vital if you are to write effective fiction.

Empathising with the reader

The illusion story about Jeff and Liz works for two reasons:

1.   A large section of the readership will have teenage sons.

2.   The same age group will also have widowed or divorced parents.

Involving the reader

As the story progresses, the female reader's sympathies will be moving from one character to the other. On the one hand, the reader will understand how a mother feels when her son is about to leave the nest. On the other, she will be sympathetic towards a young boy's romantic plight.

If the story is written with enough sensitivity, the reader will become so involved in resolving the problem that it will not occur to her that the characters could be anything other than mother and son.

However, when the final twist is revealed, she will have no difficulty in relating to the true situation, a father announcing to an adult daughter his intention to remarry.

USING FAMILIAR SETTINGS AND SITUATIONS

As we have seen, the example above is a familiar situation for many families who fall into a particular age category.

Similarly, other age groups will identify with specific locations. To illustrate the point, try a quick association test by writing down the sexes and age groups that immediately come to mind in the following settings:

1. Supermarket
2. Office
3. School gates
4. Bus
5. Disco
6. Gym
7. Evening class
8. Commuter train
9. Kitchen
10. Allotment

If the word 'allotment' conjures up a picture of a retired, male pensioner tending his vegetables, think how his ordered existence might be turned upside down if the neighbouring plot was taken by a young, well-heeled career woman.

The art of twist story writing is to take familiar settings and situations and turn them on their heads.

Who are you appealing to?

When you write a story for the women's magazine market, you want your reader to relate to the surroundings you are depicting.

The magazines of the 1990s inform, involve and offer a ray of hope to women who are working hard to make ends meet and keep families together. Their gossipy format ensures entertainment value, particularly from true life tales and, increasingly, celebrity interviews but they are not designed to whisk the reader off into a fantasy world where everything is bathed in a rosy glow.

Realistic escapism
The twist story reflects the hopes, dreams and wishes of the readership in a way that is totally different from the standard romance.

In a romance, the heroine invariably resolves her difficulties in such a way that she can look forward to a life of bliss with her ideal man, so creating some enchanting but pretty unrealistic expectations.

In a twist story, the central character takes whatever action she or he has to in order to turn an instantly recognisable situation to his or her best advantage.

In other words, romances depict life as we would like it to be whilst twist stories take a far more down-to-earth approach.

MAKING YOUR READER CARE

The importance of caring about your characters cannot be over-emphasised. Remember that if **you** don't care, neither will your reader.

Shedding real tears
In common with actors who assume the role of the characters they play, many writers become so involved with their characters that they share their emotions as they set them down on the page.

You may feel this is a bit over the top for a 1,200-word twist in the tale but if you've put enough into your characters, relating to their feelings is unavoidable. If the emotive passage you've just written reduces you to tears when you read it back, congratulations! You're definitely on the right track.

Fighting for your rights
Fiction writers draw on their own personal experiences for story ideas and the following scenario will strike a chord with anyone who worked hard in their youth to save up for the things they wanted:

A young boy has run errands and saved up his pocket money for months to buy a bike. He is proudly riding it home when he is confronted by the leader of a local gang who taunts and chases him along the road.

The boy locks his bike in the garden shed for safety but that night the shed is broken into and the bike is stolen. Everyone knows it was the gang but they can't prove a thing. Two days later, the boy sees the gangleader riding round on his bike. He confronts him but the thief is older and stronger. The boy is knocked down and has to watch helplessly as the thief pedals away.

Touching a nerve

The story contains a number of elements which should touch the emotions of most adults. For example:

- Anyone who has owned a bike will know that there is a good chance someone will want to steal it.

- Anyone who has saved hard for an expensive item will be extremely possessive about it.

- Parents will feel strongly about a child being hurt, either physically or emotionally.

- Anyone who has been bullied will relate to the boy's pain.

- Anyone who has experienced a burglary will identify with the boy's loss.

CLOSING LINES

Bringing the story to a satisfactory close can be quite difficult. Even when you have the closing line in your mind at the start, by the time you've finished the story, it may not work nearly so well as you thought it would when you began

When planning your closing line, bear in mind that it should perform the following functions:

- tie up the loose ends
- summarise the plot
- reveal or reinforce the twist.

Tying all the loose ends

If the construction of the story has gone the way you planned it, then the last line will come naturally. There should be no loose ends left by the time you come to reveal the twist.

If there are one or two unexplained events, then you've probably wandered away from the main storyline and you should look again at the story's content.

Summarising the plot

The last line should summarise everything that has gone before. It should have an element of flourish in it, making the point that everything has turned out just as it was planned.

The effect you are working towards in a twist story is one of approval from the reader. You want the reader to say 'Of course! I should have realised that right from the start.'

No matter how dark the tone of the story, you want to leave the reader with at least the hint of a satisfied smile on their lips. Now everything has been made clear to them, they can see how it was right from the beginning.

For example, at the beginning of Joyce Begg's story, 'Still Waters', Charles Teddington's wife is described as having a 'Mona Lisa smile'. As the story progresses, it is revealed that Charles' bright, clever and beloved daughter who, he thankfully boasts, takes after him rather than her insignificant mother is not, in fact, his child at all.

Refusing to name the girl's real father, the wife's closing line not only sums up her contempt for her spiteful husband but also brings the story to a very satisfactory close:

> *But she had said her piece, and said no more. The Mona Lisa smile was firmly back in place.*
>
> ('Still Waters', *Woman's Realm*, 1993)

We know very early on that the wife is hiding something but the revelation about the daughter's parentage brings about a satisfying shift in the balance of power within the couple's relationship.

Revealing the twist

In a twist story, the last line should be the one which not only ties up all the loose ends but also reveals the twist.

In her story 'Unnecessary Risk', Marion Naylor puts her characteristically wicked sense of humour to excellent use.

A Glaswegian couple is drifting in a stolen canoe on the grey waters of a Scottish loch. An unlikely pair to be admiring the scenery, it soon becomes clear that they are scanning the shore for isolated houses to rob.

They strike lucky when, almost by accident, they stumble across the week's takings of a lakeside hotel. Scanning the lake for a suitable hiding place for the loot, they see a small, barren island where they stash their haul before making rapidly for the shore.

They return the next day to be faced with nothing but a vast expanse of grey water. The island has gone. The reason for its disappearance is revealed right at the end with the following last line:

And fruitlessly, with steadily blistering hands, he went on paddling backwards and forwards with growing desperation across the grey all-concealing waters of Loch Ness.

('Unnecessary Risk', *Bella* 1995)

CASE STUDIES

Rosemary disapproves of today's young women

Rosemary is a good, imaginative writer, but well into her sixties and with no children of her own, she finds it difficult to relate to young people.

She has had several non-fiction articles published in magazines aimed at the retirement market but her disapproving attitude towards young women comes through in all her fiction writing. Unless she can overcome this prejudice, she will continue to experience difficulty in writing for the magazine market.

Carol utilises her own experiences

Carol is a single woman in her early twenties. She has a responsible office job in town and travels to work every day by tube. The story she is writing is centred around a vicious psychopath pursuing a young woman after dark in the city.

In order to portray her intended victim's reactions realistically, Carol draws on her own reactions and emotions when working late and travelling home at night.

She knows only too well how the atmosphere in her office changes once her colleagues have left the building and how a lone woman feels travelling in the evening on almost deserted tubes and stations. Using her own experiences, she has no difficulty conveying the threatening atmosphere in a deserted office building and on the underground train with terrifying realism.

CHECKLIST

1. Do you care what happens to your characters?

2. Has the point you wanted to make come over clearly?

3. Have you created the illusion you intended?

4. Will your reader be satisfied with the outcome?

5. Are the characters and setting relevant to your intended readership?

6. Does your closing line tie up all the loose ends?

ASSIGNMENT

Pick the incident you most closely identify with from the list below and use it as a theme for a story:

1. A child being punished for something it didn't do.

2. Not being picked to join a group or team.

3. A teenage boy laughed at by the girl he asks to dance.

4. A teenage girl snubbed by the boy she adores.

5. An embarrassing incident during a job interview.

6. Saying or doing something naïve on your first day at work.

7. Meeting with opposition when trying to get a refund for faulty goods.

8. Being treated with contempt by an officious person.

9. Being passed over for promotion.

10. Waiting patiently for a car parking space only to have someone nip into it before you can get your car into reverse.

8
Writing to Editorial Requirements

WORKING WITHIN THE SHORT STORY FORMAT

The Concise Oxford Dictionary defines the short story as being:

'of the character of a novel but less length'.

The essential elements of fiction

Whilst a magazine short story highlights one incident in the life of a central character, the essential elements of a fictional story must also be included, i.e.:

- characters
- background
- setting
- conflict
- a sense of time
- a beginning, middle and a satisfactory end.

Without these ingredients, the story will have no substance. However, in order to include them, you may find yourself writing far more than you had ever intended, so how do you know what to discard and what to retain?

Selecting an incident

A story should always begin at the point where something unusual is about to happen.

However, whilst in a novel there is room to go back and describe the background leading up to this event and to move on and explore the long-term consequences, a magazine short story is more firmly set in the 'here and now'.

It is up to the writer to select an incident from the character's life which has enough substance to capture the reader's interest and sustain a twisted plot.

Applying the techniques of fiction writing

In previous chapters, we have looked at the function of flashback, dialogue and interaction in providing the reader with background information and a sense of what is to come.

All these techniques must be brought into play when writing a magazine story so that the reader knows enough about the central character's history to appreciate the twist in the tale.

However, the fiction writer must have sufficient empathy with his or her characters to reveal, almost unconsciously, little snippets of information through the way they interact with one another.

For example, in Fred Clayson's story, 'Breaking Even', Bob Harris, the central character, is clearly in deep financial trouble. He is also the strong, silent type, unwilling to let his wife know exactly how bad things have become, as the following extract illustrates:

> *His wife, Carol, placed a calming hand on his shoulder. Gently, she massaged the tenseness from his knotted neck muscles, 'You shouldn't worry so much. We'll pull through eventually. Remember, they can't get money out of us if we haven't got any.'*
>
> *Bob kissed her hand gently and fought down the desire to shout. Didn't she know it was his job on the line – their house at risk? The thought of being without either was killing him; the neighbours would have a field day gossiping.*
>
> ('Breaking Even', Fred Clayson, *Bella* 1995)

Fred expertly paints a picture of a caring man at the end of his tether. He skilfully guides the reader to the conclusion that, however drastic the action he takes, Bob's good character will not allow him to do anything inherently bad.

RINGING SEASONAL CHANGES

Original stories with a clear seasonal theme are welcomed with open arms by magazine editors. If you can come up with a bright, new idea for Christmas, Valentine's Day or Halloween, or simply create a convincing atmosphere for any one of the four seasons, your story will stand a slightly better than average chance of acceptance.

Planning ahead

It's easy to think of Christmas plots when the nights are drawing in and the shops are full of cards and decorations. Unfortunately, if you wait for that jolly seasonal feel, you'll be far too late for the magazine market.

Keeping to lead times

In order for your story to be considered for a seasonal slot, keep a note of lead times, the timespan required for editorial planning. Below is a rough guide to when you should submit a seasonal manuscript:

- Weekly magazines   3–4 months ahead

- Monthly magazines   6–9 months ahead

Bear in mind that the same rules should be applied to stories with a summer holiday theme or those set firmly in the middle of winter.

WRAPPING UP THE STORY

Each writer will have their own method of working. Some will work to a set plan of the story. Others will write it as it comes, but whichever method you choose, it is important to ensure that the story is written to its required length.

Working to strict requirements

An editor has a specific slot to fill and has no time either to cut or to add paragraphs in order to make your story fit the space allotted.

The techniques applied in cutting your work will be explored in more detail later in this chapter. However, if your story comes up short, it is extremely likely that you've left out one or more vital ingredients.

If your 850-word story only comes to 500 words, ask yourself the following questions:

1. What have I left out?

2. Is the characterisation strong enough?

3. Have I included sufficient description?

4. Is there sufficient background information?

5. Have I achieved a satisfactory twist?

6. Is there sufficient substance to the story?

Counting the pages

Writing to length is a skill that, like any other, improves with practice. Once you've done it a few times, you begin to know where you are in the story and where to start wrapping it up. You may wish to use the following as a guide:

1 x	A4 page of typed double-line spacing						=	approx	250 words
2 x	"	"	"	"	"	"	"	=	approx	500 words
3 x	"	"	"	"	"	"	"	=	approx	850 words
4 x	"	"	"	"	"	"	"	=	approx	1,000 words
5 x	"	"	"	"	"	"	"	=	approx	1,200 words

These estimated figures vary depending on the typewriter or word processor you use but you will soon get to know the idiosyncrasies of your own machine so that, when you reach a certain page in your manuscript, you will know that you are running out of wordage.

CHOOSING A TITLE

Many writers agonise for hours over their choice of title, only to find that the story appears in print under a totally different heading.

You should look upon the title as a label by which the reader can gain an insight into the story's theme at a single glance. Remember that the wording has to fit the space provided, so keep it short and snappy.

Try to limit the number of words to an absolute minimum. One or two word headings which sum up the tone of the story and have immediate impact will be the most likely to find favour with an editor. The following selection of titles from my own published stories may help to give you a clearer picture of the sort of headings editors like to use:

Twist titles

● **'Cleaning Up'** About a young cleaner who turns the tables on the egotistical, selfish couple who employ her to clean their sumptuous home. (*Best* 1990)

● **'Quiet Life'** About a mother whose son uses her as an excuse for breaking off any potentially serious relationship. (*Woman's Realm* 1994)

- **'Will Power'**   About an elderly lady who decides to make a rather unusual will. (*Bella* 1995)

GUESSING THE TWIST

Time after time, a reader will wave a magazine under your nose and smugly tell you that they guessed the twist in the first line of the tale.

If your story is well-constructed, neither the reader nor the editor should be able to guess the twist. However, to quote Abraham Lincoln:

> *'You can fool some of the people all of the time and all of the people some of the time but you cannot fool all of the people all of the time.'*

REACHING A BROAD READERSHIP

Even those magazines which are specifically targeted at a limited age and social group will still attract a very broad range of readers.

A proportion of the readers will never guess the twist, whilst another section always will. Your task is to reach as many as you can of the first group and hope that your story at least entertains the second.

Fiction editors are always on the lookout for well-written, original plots. It is unlikely that anything you can come up with in the way of a twist will be absolutely new to them but they will know immediately whether or not your story will appeal to their readership.

WHAT IS THE FICTION EDITOR LOOKING FOR?

Pat Richardson, Fiction Editor of *Best* has the following checklist for submissions:

- **Interest**   so I can get beyond the second paragraph without boredom

- **Involvement** so I can relate to the characters.

- **Intrigue**   so I care what happens.

- **Originality** so I haven't heard it before.

- **Surprise**   so I don't guess the ending.

- **Satisfaction**   so I'm convinced by and pleased with the outcome. Also means the story scores well on all the above points. No 'it doesn't work'; no 'second thoughts'. Best of all, a story one will keep and read again, recommend. After all, that's what, as Fiction Editor, I do.

(Pat Richardson, Fiction Editor, *Best*)

EDITORIAL GUIDELINES

Because market requirements are constantly changing, not all editors are prepared to issue fiction guidelines. The stories currently published in the magazines are by far your best indication of style, characters and content.

The magazines listed below all publish twist in the tale stories and will all send you editorial guidelines on receipt of a stamped, addressed envelope (sae):

- *Bella*
- *Best*
- *Chat*
- *My Weekly*
- *Take A Break*
- *That's Life*
- *Woman's Weekly*

The information you receive ranges from a brief, friendly, standard letter to a comprehensive 4-page document, but all editorial guidelines advise would-be contributors to:

read the magazine before you attempt to write for it.

This advice sounds obvious but it is clear from the comments made by the editors who have contributed to this book that their postbags contain a large number of totally unsuitable manuscripts.

No matter how much or how little information they are prepared to give freelance contributors, the editors are all looking for the same thing. Well-written, neatly presented manuscripts reflecting the lives of their readers and the style of their magazine.

ASSESSING YOUR OWN WORK

One of the most difficult aspects of writing is developing the ability to assess your own work.

When you sat down to write the story, you knew what the ending would be. Having the plot firmly in your mind from the start, you have done your best to conceal the true facts from the reader.

You now have to judge whether you have succeeded and in order to do this, you have to read the story as though it has been written by someone else.

Criticising your story

It is tempting to ask family and friends for their opinion but this is not always wise. Comments will range from the extremely enthusiastic to the hyper-critical and it is difficult to decide which is the worse option.

By far the most competent people to judge your work are yourself and an editor. A fellow writer can offer you invaluable support but unless you are prepared to train yourself to criticise your own writing, you will find it difficult to obtain an unbiased, expert opinion.

Building self-confidence

Confidence in your own ability is the key to self-assessment. If you love reading and writing stories, then it should only be a short step to criticising your own work.

Try to avoid being over-critical. If you tinker with a story too much, you can destroy it. Listed below are a few suggestions which you may find helpful:

- As soon as the story is completed, put it away and do something else for a few hours.

- Mull the whole thing over in your mind to iron out any blips.

- Take a deep breath and relax before reading the story through.

- Read the story as though it is the first time you've ever seen it.

CUTTING YOUR STORY TO LENGTH

One of the most useful rules every writer should remember is:

Never use two words when one will do.

However, simply cutting out the odd word here and there will not necessarily offer the required solution.

Cutting and tightening

Sometimes, the excess wordage is caused not by what you say but by how you say it. By rephrasing something or turning it around, you can often cut the number of words by half. For example:

The rain was beating hard against the window panes, causing the frames to rattle and the huge droplets to gather in such volume that water began to run down the walls and onto the ground below.

(36 words)

This can be effectively cut by more than half the original wordage whilst retaining the required sense and atmosphere.

Huge droplets of rain rattled the window panes, streaming down the walls to the ground below.

(16 words)

Passages of purple prose

Love of language can be as much of a curse to the short story writer as a blessing. An articulate author renowned for their extensive vocabulary can find the disciplines of short story writing very restrictive.

Well aware of this problem, Dr Samuel Johnson offered the following advice to authors:

'Read over your compositions and wherever you meet with a passage which you think is particularly fine, strike it out.'

Writing for magazines requires the use of language which is quick to read and easy to understand. Sentences should be short and to the point, dialogue fast moving with passages of description kept to a minimum.

If the muse takes hold and purple passages begin to flow, take Dr Johnson's advice and strike them out.

CHECKLIST

1.   Have you selected an incident with sufficient substance for a story?

2.   Can you give it a seasonal slant?

3.   Are you submitting it in good time?

4.   Have you read it through with a critical eye?

5.   Is the story the required length?

6.   Did you improve the story when you cut it?

ASSIGNMENT

Cut and tighten the following passage in a way that retains the sense of urgency without losing any of the detail:

> *He pressed down hard on the brake but was horrified to find that it did not work. As they were travelling on a steep mountain road, the car began to gather speed, moving faster and faster until, to his dismay, he saw that they were approaching a highly dangerous bend.*
>
> (50 words)

(For suggested rewrite, see p. 116)

9
Submitting Your Manuscript to an Editor

CONTACTING EDITORS

If you've done your market research thoroughly, you will be writing for a magazine which you enjoy reading and which has stated that unsolicited manuscripts will be considered.

Beating the competition

Depending on the content and style of the magazine, including the ones which do not publish fiction, editors receive anything from 10 to 900 unsolicited *fiction* manuscripts per month.

In order to give you a clearer picture, the table in Fig. 5 shows the approximate number of manuscripts received per month and the approximate number purchased by a selection of magazines which are prepared to consider unsolicited fiction.

Getting to know the editor

At first sight, the competition appears quite daunting but you can take comfort from the fact that a very large proportion of unsolicited manuscripts are totally unsuitable for publication.

An editor will, therefore, be delighted to receive a manuscript which shows that you have analysed the magazine and identified the kind of fiction most likely to appeal to its readership.

You also should be aware that there are some topics magazines tend to avoid. As a general rule, taboo subjects are:

- religion
- politics
- racism
- explicit sex and/or violence.

Editors are people too

Just like you and me, editors have their good and bad days. Despite

Publication	Unsolicited fiction submissions received per month	Number purchased (where available)
Bella	900	6–7 per year
Best	200	50 per year
Chat	200–300	(Not available but most of the fiction purchased is from unsolicited submissions)
My Weekly	400	16–20 per month (not all twists)
That's Life!	100	7 per month
Woman	80	1 per week
Woman & Home	200–300	5–6 per year
Woman's Weekly	600	1–2 per month

Fig. 5. Unsolicited fiction submissions to UK magazines.

exceptionally heavy workloads, they can often be very approachable and quick to recognise and encourage new talent. They do, however, loathe being constantly pestered on the telephone or being expected to consider totally unsuitable manuscripts.

Listed below is a selection of comments from editors of leading magazines. *Please note that not all of these publications feature twist in the tale stories.*

The question **'what causes you most irritation?'** elicited the following replies:

- Badly presented copy – not at all our style – where readers obviously haven't read our magazine to see what we require. (June Hammond, *Woman*. Twist slot.)

- Pomposity in writing – also those writers who do not look at the magazine before sending in material. The magazine is the best possible guide to what is acceptable. (Neil Patrick, *Yours*. No twist slot.)

- Unconvincing words, actions, dialogue. An unlikely plot 'excused' by an 'it was all a dream' scenario. Bad spelling. (Pat Richardson, *Best*. Twist slot.)

- Long sentences, too much description. Manuscripts which aren't double-line spaced. Stories which are too long. Fiction which is described as twist in the tale but has no twist or a very weak twist at the end. (Emma Fabian, *That's Life*. Twist slot.)

- Requests for guidance on style – writers should refer to the magazine and use initiative. (Lucy Bulmer, *Prima*. No fiction.)

- Submissions which show the writer has not studied the magazine to find out who the reader is. (Kati Nicholl, *Woman & Home*. Twists accepted but no specific slot.)

- Stories where the outcome is obvious from the outset. Contrived endings, 'It was all just a dream'. Stories which 'tell' rather than 'show'. (Gaynor Davies, *Woman's Weekly*. Twist slot.)

- Writers who have clearly not studied the market. Being called 'Mr'. Contributors who insist on sending more than three stories at a time.

J. Smith
5 The Laurels, Newtown AA1 1AA
Tel: (0123) 456789

ACCEPTANCE

A short story of approx 1,200 words
by
Jane Smith

Fig. 6. Sample front sheet.

People who do not enclose SAEs. Badly typed manuscripts. (Shelley Silas, *Chat*. Twist slot.)

● Well-used plotlines, sloppy writing. (Linda O'Byrne, *Bella*. Twist slot.)

● Self-indulgent, badly constructed 'arty' stories written by people showing patent disregard for the intended market and stories set in the 1800s about housekeepers and handsome landowners. (Ian Sommerville, *My Weekly*. Some twist stories.)

PRESENTING YOUR MANUSCRIPT

As stated in the above comments, a good way to annoy editors is to present them with a poorly laid-out, badly written manuscript.

Make sure that your manuscript is clear and easy to read. Each page should bear the story's title, author's name and page number and you may wish to put 'contd./. . .' or 'm.f. . .' and the next page number at the foot of your pages to indicate where more is to follow.

Front sheet

It is also helpful if you include a 'front sheet' bearing your name and address, the story's title and the approximate number of words. If you are using a pen-name, this should also appear on the front sheet, as illustrated in Fig. 6.

Covering letter

A brief covering letter addressed to the editor by name should also accompany your manuscript. This will not only help the editor keep track of your work but is a matter of courtesy which, providing you keep it short and to the point, is appreciated by the person with whom you wish to build a good working relationship.

As you can see from the sample covering letter in Fig. 7, the story's title should be included as an extra safeguard to help keep track of your work.

If you decide to use a pen-name, to avoid confusion, be sure to make your real name clear to the editor. Failure to do so could result in you being unable to cash a payment cheque made out to your fictitious alter ego.

The do's and don'ts of presentation

Avoid causing irritation and confusion to prospective editors by taking the following precautions:

J. Smith
5 The Laurels, Newtown AA1 1AA
Tel: (0123) 456789

1 July 19XX

Susan Jones
Fiction Editor
The Magazine
Fleet Street
London EC4

Dear Susan Jones

Please find enclosed a short story of approximately 1,200 words entitled 'ACCEPTANCE' which I hope you will find suitable for *The Magazine*'s twist story slot.

I have enclosed return postage for your convenience and look forward to hearing from you.

Yours sincerely

J. Smith

Encl:

Fig. 7. Sample covering letter.

- **Do** type your manuscript clearly in double-line spacing on one side only of white A4-size paper.

- **Don't** ever submit handwritten manuscripts.

- **Do** include a front sheet bearing your name and address.

- **Don't** forget to number and head each page of your story.

- **Do** address your (brief) covering letter to the fiction editor by name.

- **Don't** telephone the editor to discuss your ideas.

- **Do** include return postage.

- **Don't** telephone the editor the next day to see if your manuscript has arrived.

- **Do** accept the editor's decision.

- **Don't** telephone the editor to ask what was wrong with your story.

- **Do** follow any advice given in a rejection letter.

- **Don't** let rejection get you down.

Using new ribbons

If your word processor has a dot matrix printer, bear in mind that printing out on the 'Draft Quality' setting using an elderly fabric ribbon is a false economy.

Such cost-conscious writers have only themselves to blame for the fact that many editors today refuse to consider manuscripts produced on dot matrix printers. A busy editor faced with the prospect of trying to decipher faint print under artificial light will, understandably, give up in disgust.

Checking your spelling

It is easy to tell when a writer has used their word processor's spellcheck facility to correct their spelling mistakes.

Unless you have a state of the art machine with the very latest software, your spellchecker will only tell you if the spelling of the word you have typed is correct, not if it is in context.

For example, in a story set in a medieval castle, one of the guards was described as having a '*steal* helmet'. The spellcheck was perfectly happy with this, even though the correct spelling was, of course, *steel*.

If you are unsure of the spelling of any word, look it up in a dictionary. Never rely on your spellcheck program.

Punctuating for publication

Punctuation performs certain vital functions:

- It denotes speech.

- It denotes sentences.

- It puts emphasis in the correct places.

- It makes sense of the story.

Your punctuation need not be grammatically perfect but it must fulfil the functions listed above.

Editors will always forgive occasional spelling, punctuation and typing errors. However, if any or all of these three components are particularly poor, it will be an indication that the writer lacks the basic grammatical skills necessary to write for publication.

CHASING UP MISSING MANUSCRIPTS

The time editors take to contact writers depends very much on their workload and the popularity of the magazine. Try not to be too impatient to discover the fate of your story – a long wait may mean the editor is seriously considering its purchase.

Getting to the top of the 'slush pile'

The 'slush pile' is the unsavoury title given to the unsolicited manuscripts awaiting the perusal of an editor. Whilst you can be assured that your manuscript will eventually be read, each editor has their own system for prioritising submissions.

A clean, well-presented manuscript of the right thickness, addressed to the right person, will probably find its way to the top of the slush pile rather more quickly than its scruffy, well-thumbed counterpart.

Writing chase-up letters

As a general rule, give your story around six to eight weeks before you think about chasing it up. Bear in mind, however, that some magazines can take as long as three months to consider a manuscript.

Address your letter personally to the editor, giving the name of the story, the date you sent it and confirming that return postage was included.

As you can see from the example in Fig. 8, the letter should be short and to the point and avoid giving deadlines for the story's return or it may come winging back before the glue is dry on your envelope.

Give it a good seven days before you resort to telephoning and always be polite. You will find it yields much better results and the magazine's clerical staff will usually go out of their way to help you.

INVOICING AND COPYRIGHT

Acceptance will not necessarily come in the form of a letter. Some editors prefer to telephone contributors to give them the good news and will throw a payment figure casually into the conversation.

Negotiating a deal

Different magazines have different rates of pay. Some will have a predetermined pay scale, depending on the writer's experience. Others will simply pay a standard fee.

The offer will usually include details of the rights the editor wishes to purchase. You can accept or decline the offer but negotiation is rare.

Bear in mind that you are in a buyer's market and if you won't accept the terms on offer, the editor can always find another writer who will.

Establishing copyright

Most writers will be hoping to sell their work on a 'First British Serial Rights' (FBSR) basis. This means that you retain overall copyright in the work but the magazine has the right to publish your story once and only in the UK.

Some authors like to mark their manuscripts with the copyright term 'FBSR' before they submit them for publication but there is little point in doing this.

Different magazine editors like to purchase different rights and the offers they make depend upon a variety of factors, including your own previous writing experience.

J. Smith
5 The Laurels, Newtown AA1 1AA
Tel: (0123) 456789

20 August 19XX

Susan Jones
Fiction Editor
The Magazine
Fleet Street
London EC4

Dear Susan Jones

At the beginning of last month, I submitted a story entitled 'ACCEPTANCE' for your consideration, together with return postage.

To date, I have heard nothing from you and would be grateful if you could let me know whether my story is suitable for *The Magazine*.

I look forward to hearing from you.

Yours sincerely

Jane Smith

Fig. 8. Sample chase up letter.

Offers will, therefore, range from 'FBSR' for one year only to UK and specified foreign rights and even 'All World Rights For All Purposes', which means that you will be giving up all title to your work.

Keeping track of your copyright

Keep careful note of the copyright you have sold. A story published 'FBSR' can be offered for sale anywhere else in the world and on a second, third, etc. basis in the UK.

You must, therefore, have a comprehensive record of where and on what copyright basis your stories have been sold.

Invoicing

Once an offer has been made, you may be asked for an invoice. As you can see from the example in Fig. 9, this should bear your own name, address, the figure agreed and the rights purchased. Remember that, if you have used a pen-name, you must ensure that the magazine's accounts department is well aware of your real name for the purposes of making out the cheques.

In some instances, the editor may quote a figure over the telephone and once accepted, a cheque will arrive attached to an acceptance slip specifying the rights being purchased. This can be anything from 'FBSR' to 'All Rights for All Purposes' but the cheque cannot be cashed unless the slip is signed. This is perfectly legal but the practice is under ongoing scrutiny from the National Union of Journalists (NUJ).

Payment on acceptance

Most reputable publishers authorise payment as soon as you have agreed to sell them your manuscript. It may take quite a while for the cheque to work its way through the system but it will probably arrive before your story appears in the magazine.

Payment on publication

Some editors pay on publication and this can mean that the story is kept on file for an unacceptably long period.

Under these circumstances, you may eventually have to face the fact that the story is never going to be published in this particular magazine and take steps to retrieve it from the editor or try to negotiate a 'kill fee', i.e. a one-off payment in full and final settlement. Guidelines on how to go about this are available from the NUJ, Acorn House, 314 Gray's Inn Road, London WC1X 8DP. Tel: (0171) 278 7916.

J. Smith
5 The Laurels, Newtown AA1 1AA
Tel: (0123) 456789

INVOICE

1 September 19XX

The Magazine
Fleet Street
London EC4

To

A short story of approx 1,200 words entitled ACCEPTANCE

First British Serial Rights
(as agreed with Susan Jones)   £150

Fig. 9. Sample invoice.

SYNDICATING YOUR WORK

The magazines featured in this book are all based in the UK but there are, of course, markets for short stories abroad.

Exactly the same rules apply when sending your work to overseas editors but return postage should be in the form of sufficient 'International Reply Coupons' (IRCs) to cover the full cost of returning your manuscript to the UK. IRCs can be obtained from any post office.

In the UK, magazine editors rarely buy stories from syndication agents but for writers who have built up a large portfolio of work, syndication may offer a viable method of selling stories abroad.

A good agency will have a wide knowledge of overseas markets and the percentage they take could well outweigh the cost of producing copies, market research and postage to foreign magazines.

Lists of reputable syndication agencies, with details of the material they handle, can be found in the *Writers' & Artists' Yearbook* (A & C Black), together with a warning to **'make preliminary enquiries before submitting MSS to ascertain terms of work.'**

It is important to compare the commission rates of a selection of agencies and you will also need to establish the length of time over which they are prepared to offer your work for sale.

OUTGOINGS AND INCOME

All copies of your invoices and payments slips must be carefully filed for both record-keeping and tax purposes.

Notifying the Inland Revenue

Publishing houses will all record the payments made to you for tax purposes and you will be required to declare any income you make from your writing to the Inland Revenue.

However, legitimate expenses you incur in producing work for publication may be offset against tax.

Requesting receipts

Every time you make a writing-related purchase, ask for a receipt and place it on file. Your biggest outlay will almost certainly be for the following items:

- typewriter ribbons

- ribbons, ink or toner for word processor printers

- stationery

- postage

- magazine subscriptions

- telephone calls.

There will be other expenses related to working from home which can also be legitimately offset against tax:

- word processor and/or computers

- desks

- typists' chairs

- computer discs

- fax machines

- filing cabinets.

You can also offset the cost of using a room in your home as an office and you can obtain details of self-employed tax allowances from your local Inland Revenue office.

Alternatively, you may wish to employ an accountant to handle your affairs. Charges vary, as may the quality of service. Try to obtain recommendations from other freelance writers and shop around for a good deal.

CASE STUDIES

Janet rejects editorial advice

Janet is a keen member of her local writers' circle. In her mid-forties, she has a forceful, decisive personality. She has a tendency to make snap judgements about people, a trait which is reflected in her fiction writing. When one of her manuscripts is returned with a note suggesting alterations, she refuses point blank to consider the editor's comments. As far as Janet is concerned, the story is fine and there is no need to tamper with it. So far, none of her stories have been accepted for publication.

Ted charms the editor

Ted is a middle-aged railworker who enjoys writing twist stories and submitting them to suitable markets. Although, initially, his manuscripts are not quite right for publication, his brief covering letters are so full of friendly humour, that one editor can't resist writing back personally to offer helpful advice.

Ted immediately acts on the advice given and his next manuscript is accepted for publication. He is now a regular contributor to the magazine's twist story page.

CHECKLIST

1. Have you numbered each page of your manuscript?

2. Does your name and the story's title appear on each page?

3. Is the print clear enough?

4. Have you checked that your spelling is accurate?

5. Have you included return postage?

6. Have you addressed your manuscript to the right person?

ASSIGNMENT

Correctly punctuate the following passage (answers on page 116):

Julie awoke late the following morning Oh no she cried as she leapt out of bed and rushed downstairs into the kitchen Ill lose my job if I miss the bus For Heavens sake Mum why didnt you wake me Calmly her mother carried on sipping her tea Id forget about breakfast if I were you she bit into a slice of thickly buttered toast Its too late for that but if youre quick you might have time for a shower You did this deliberately Julie snapped as she hurried towards the bathroom Did what her mother raised an innocent eyebrow Its hardly my fault if you dont get up when your alarm goes off Personally I dont know how anyone could sleep through that racket I would have thought its bell was loud enough to waken the dead

10
Rewriting for Publication

ACCEPTING EDITORIAL GUIDANCE

Mention the title 'Editor' to a group of struggling short story writers and the reaction will, to say the least, be mixed.

Writers' opinions of editorial ability vary in direct relation to the number of acceptances or rejections they have had but contrary to common belief, editors actually want your submission to be successful.

This fact is borne out not only by the helpful information leading magazine editors have been kind enough to supply for me to use in this book but also by some of the comments they have made:

- 'Good magazine fiction writers are hard to find. I'm very pleased to receive a good story. (Emma Fabian, *That's Life!*)

- 'On the whole, I welcome unsolicited manuscripts. It gives me great pleasure to buy from a writer who has never been published before.' (Shelley Silas, *Chat.*)

Giving them what they want
Knowing that editors want to hear from writers, it is up to us to give them what they want.

Editors are looking for at least one, if not all, of the following components in a manuscript:

- originality

- identity with their housestyle

- reader identification

- strong characterisation

- realism

● a good twist

● double or triple twists

● the potential to write regularly for their magazine.

Market requirements at the time of going to print are set out in the table in Fig 10. Included in the table are the number of words required, details from the editor regarding content and style of the story and where available, rates of pay and rights purchased.

Whilst a number of publications produce fiction guidelines for freelance contributors, editorial requirements change rapidly. You will learn far more about the magazine's requirements by studying recent editions of the magazine, than by relying solely on editorial guidelines.

Acting on editorial advice

Good short story writers are few and far between. Skilled twist writers are an even rarer commodity. Once you have demonstrated an ability to write a twist in the tale, editors will be keen to develop your potential.

All writers are familiar with the dreaded rejection slip but occasionally, a manuscript is returned with a letter asking for alterations which might make it suitable for publication.

At this stage, no formal offer will have been made but if you've got this close, it makes sense to rewrite the story along the suggested lines and re-submit it.

REWORKING YOUR STORY

At first sight, the suggestion may seem trivial or out of step with your own thinking. You may feel resentful that the editor does not trust your artistic judgement.

If so, you might benefit from this advice from short story writer E. Evans:

'Occasionally an editor will come back to me and say they liked the story but could I change this/put in that/alter the ending or whatever. I've never had any problem with this approach – it is, after all, their magazine.'

It is no coincidence that twist, mystery and romantic stories by this

Publication	Contact	Twist slot	No. of words	Rates of pay and rights purchased	Requirements
Bella 25–27 Camden Road London NW1 9LL Tel: (0171) 284 0909	Linda O'Byrne Fiction Editor	Mini Mystery	1,200	From £160 FBSR	Originality – sharpness of thought and style. Crisp writing, more originality. Ability to think sideways.
Best 10th Floor, Portland House, Stag Place London SW1E 5AU Tel: (0171) 245 8833	Pat Richardson Fiction Editor	5 Minute Fiction	1,300	£100 First UK for 2 years	Originality, interest, involvement intrigue, surprise, satisfaction. Characters that readers will identify with, convincing action. and dialogue.
Chat King's Reach Tower Stamford St London SE1 9LS Tel: (0171) 261 5000	Shelly Silas Fiction Editor	Short Story	800–900	From £80 FBSR	Originality, good writing, an awareness of the market, humour. A well-presented story. Simplicity. Stories that are too complicated or too clever usually fail to arouse interest.
My Weekly D.C. Thomson & Co. Ltd. 80 Kingsway East Dundee DD4 8SL Tel: (01382) 223 131	Ian Sommerville Fiction Editor	Short Stories (No specific twist slot)	500–2,500	Negotiable FBSR	Heartwarming, emotional (i.e. humour or pathos) stories centred around credible characters with whom readers can identify. Stories should entertain and end on a hopeful note. Mostly they are contemporary.
Take a Break 25–27 Camden Road London NW1 9LL Tel: (0171) 284 0909	Norah McGrath Fiction Editor	Coffee Break Fiction	1,100	£300 FBSR	Contemporary stories aimed at women from their mid-twenties upwards. A strong plot and good twist in the tale. The twist should arise out of the story rather than from a detail kept from the reader. Settings and situations which the reader can relate to.

Fig. 10. UK magazines currently taking twist stories.

Publication	Contact	Twist slot	No. of words	Rates of pay and rights purchased	Requirements
That's Life! St Martin's House (7th Floor) 140 Tottenham Court Rd London W1 9LN Tel: (0171) 388 6269	Emma Fabian	Sting in the Tale	1,000	£300 FBSR	Sharp, punchy, modern style. Story told by a woman about a woman from female viewpoint. Romance or spicy love interest.
The Lady 39–40 Bedford St London WC2E 9ER Tel: (0171) 379 4717	Beverly Davies	No specific twist slot	2,000	Variable	Humour, structure, suitable for *The Lady*.
Woman IPC Magazines King's Reach Tower Stamford Street London SE1 9LS Tel: (0171) 261 5000	June Hammond	Quick Read	1,000	FBSR, rate undisclosed	Typed, double-line spacing. Modern situations and characters. Variety of subjects that readers can identify with. Optimistic feel.
Woman & Home King's Reach Tower Stamford Street London SE1 9LS Tel: (0171) 261 5000	Kati Nicholl	No specific twist slot	Variable	FBSR, variable rate	Quality of writing, development of plot, depth of characterisation.
Woman's Weekly IPC Magazines King's Reach Tower Stamford Street London SE1 9LS Tel: (0171) 261 5000	Gaynor Davies Fiction Editor	Coffee Break Read	1,000	FBSR	A compelling story with warmth at its heart and enough conflict to keep the reader turning the pages. Romance welcome but not essential. Humour also welcome.

skilled author appear regularly on the pages of the major women's weeklies.

Thinking positively

If an editor has taken time out of a very busy working day to write and ask you to rework your story, there must be a good reason for the revisions. If nothing else, you can be confident that the editor:

- is the expert in what the reader wants

- likes your writing style

- feels you have potential

- wants to publish the story

- is prepared to give you advice and support.

Fred Clayson, a regular contributor to *Bella*'s 'Mini Mystery' slot is in no doubt about the benefits of being offered editorial advice:

> 'I must own up and say, right away, that my little success is, in no small measure, due to the help I receive from Linda (O'Byrne). She is always ready to offer advice and suggest improvements – and I gladly accept any criticism she doles out.'

Taking suggestions on board

Armed with expert advice from the editor, carefully analyse your story and see how you can turn it around to accommodate the suggested changes.

Careful cutting and tightening will allow you to move paragraphs around whilst keeping the basic storyline intact. Both Fred Clayson and E. Evans admit to being scribblers, jotting down ideas on scraps of paper.

They find the process of simply putting pen to paper a therapeutic one which not only provides them with notes from which to rework their stories but invariably leads to new story ideas.

MONITORING YOUR SUBJECT MATTER

When the twist story first began to appear in women's magazines, the content was quite tough and hard hitting.

Just a few of the more controversial topics which have been featured in twist story slots over the past eight years are:

- child molestation and murder

- post-natal depression

- children and adults with physical and mental disabilities

- armed robbery.

Handling sensitive topics

It is essential when writing about difficult areas of people's lives that the material is handled very sensitively indeed.

The twist must never revolve around the fact that someone has a disability or suffers from a debilitating condition. These details must be integral to the story for the purposes of characterisation and background information and not to provide impact or to shock the reader.

Racism and religion are two more topics which should be approached with caution. Writer E. Evans makes the following observation on religion in seasonal stories:

'I always avoid any religious theme in this kind of story since it is almost bound to cause offence to someone.'

Being aware of mood changes

Whilst many writers use their work as a medium through which they can voice strongly held feelings and opinions, the main functions of women's magazines are to inform and entertain.

Within these boundaries, the twist story slot makes up part of the entertainment element and as such, offers escapism for a world-weary readership.

It has always been difficult to place a story dealing with a potentially controversial topic, particularly if the subject matter is highly sensitive, but in the current economic and social climate, it has become even more difficult to sell a story with a hardhitting theme.

Over recent years the content of the twist story has lightened, so keep a close eye on trends in the market to ensure that the stories you write reflect the need for uplifting tales offering at least a glimmer of hope or humour to the reader.

LEARNING FROM YOUR MISTAKES

When a manuscript comes thudding back through the letterbox complete with rejection slip, many writers are deterred from trying again.

Getting back on the bike

Like learning to ride a bike, the best way to achieve success when you fall off is to get straight back on again.

Busy editors simply don't have time to give you a reason for rejection but if the first magazine you tried rejects your manuscript, it may be more suitable for another one, so type out a new covering letter and send it off again.

Adopting a positive attitude

You should be submitting your manuscript only to magazines that you know will be receptive to the specific style and content of your story.

This will considerably limit your choices, as each editor will be looking for stories containing characters, settings and themes specifically aimed at their readership.

Think positively about this and before you send it off again, check through your manuscript carefully to ensure that it meets all the requirements of the next magazine.

The published authors featured in this book have offered the following helpful suggestions for coping with rejection:

'I simply tell myself it wasn't my turn today, maybe next time'. (*Joyce Begg*)

'Rejected manuscripts in A4 size envelopes look impressive in one's letterbox.' (*Fred Clayson*)

'I think if you want to write you just have to bite the bullet, keep sending stories out and deal with the rejections philosophically (the old "they'll be sorry when I win the Booker Prize" syndrome).' (*E. Evans*)

Reading the rejection

If your manuscript has been returned to you, before you tear up your rejection letter, read it through carefully. It may not be as bad as you think. Some standard rejection letters invite you to send more examples of your work, as illustrated in the letter from the editor of *My Weekly* in Fig. 11.

D. C. Thomson & Co., Ltd.

Dundee   Glasgow   Manchester   London

My Weekly

80 KINGSWAY EAST, DUNDEE DD4 2SL.
Telephone: 0382 462276.
Telex: 76380.
Fax: 0382 452491.

Dear Contributor,

Many thanks for giving me the opportunity to read your material.

Unfortunately it is unsuitable for My Weekly.

I'll be pleased to see anything else you may care to send along.

Yours sincerely,

pp The Editor

Registered Address — ALBERT SQUARE, DUNDEE DD1 9QJ
(Registered in Scotland No. 5830)

Fig. 11. Rejection letter.

This is not, as some novice writers believe, a polite way of letting you down gently but a genuine desire on the part of the editor to see what you can do.

Never disappoint an editor. A letter like this means that your foot is now firmly in the door.

CHECKLIST

1. Have you met the editorial requirements?

2. Do you agree with the editor's suggested changes?

3. Can you provide what the editor wants?

4. Is your chosen magazine taking stories dealing with the topics you enjoy writing about?

5. Are you prepared to rework your stories to suit editorial requirements?

CASE STUDY

From idea to manuscript, to rewrite, to print

For some time, I had been turning a particular idea over in my head.

I was struck by the fact that the birth of royal babies, the weddings of TV soap characters, news reports of family health problems in the lives of celebrities will all attract gifts from adoring fans.

Many of the people who send these gifts can ill afford them, whilst the recipients are often extremely well-off or, as in the case of 'soap' characters, don't actually exist at all.

However, it would never occur to the people who buy these gifts to send them to those who would genuinely benefit from them. That is left to the discretion of those who receive them.

This strange quirk of human nature gave me the theme for a Christmas story, initially entitled 'A Message for Santa', which appeared in *Bella's* Mini Mystery Slot as 'Tell Santa'.

It centred around a seven-year-old girl called Amy who lives with her mother, a single parent with a full-time job. Working hard to keep a roof over their heads and food on the table, Amy's mother sometimes has no alternative but to leave the child in the care of a totally disinterested neighbour.

Left to her own devices, Amy is a regular visitor to the local department store's Christmas window display, which has at its centre a beautiful doll. Amy knows her mother could never afford to buy the doll for her but she has a card up her sleeve.

She recognises the crusty old man hired to play Santa in the store's grotto. He's a nasty piece of work but in his role as representative of the great man, Amy hopes he will pass a letter to Santa for her.

The old man has no idea what the child wants and in an effort to get rid of her, grabs a scruffy old doll from a pile of unwanted toys donated for underprivileged children. Pushing it into a carrier bag, he hides it round the back of his grotto next to an identical bag containing the brand new doll he is to present to the daughter of a wealthy local dignitary.

This was the ending to my original version:

'There's a bag for you round the back,' he hissed, 'Take it and clear off,' he shook a hairy fist in her face, 'And don't come back.'

As the first customers wandered into the toy department, Amy slipped behind the grotto to find not one but two Markhams carrier bags. She peeped in the first one but there was only a tattered rag doll inside, 'Can't be that one,' she reasoned, 'I bet it belongs to that box of old toys in the grotto.'

The large box in the second bag was neatly giftwrapped but Amy knew from its shape exactly what it was. The attached label bore the message, 'To a special little girl with the compliments of Markhams Store.'

The department was crowded now with people eagerly waiting to see Lady Catherine and her small daughter accept the toys charitably donated to underprivileged children by the store's customers. A beaming Mr Markham despatched an assistant to fetch a carrier bag from its hiding place behind the grotto.

'I'm sure your daughter will like the doll we have for her,' he whispered softly to Lady Catherine, 'It's our special line this year.'

Clutching the carrier bag close to her chest, Amy couldn't help smiling to herself as she walked unnoticed through the crowd. Mr Bleasdale was quite a nice man really. He had given her message to Santa after all.

The response from fiction editor Linda O'Byrne was, as you can see from her letter (Fig. 12), encouraging.

I telephoned her to discuss her suggestions and she explained that whilst she liked the idea, she needed a hint of 'magic' for a Christmas story.

H. Bauer Publishing

Bella

13 August 1990

Dear Adele

I've been puzzling over the Christmas story and I think I can see now where it's going wrong.

The problem is that the reader knows exactly what is going to happen. By having Mr Bleasdale put the rag doll in the carrier bag, etc. etc. there is no sense of surprise or mystery when Amy gets the wrong doll. I have got to have a twist at the end of the story and I haven't got one at present.

I don't know if you can see any way around this, or any other surprise ending to the story. It's so nice except for this problem at the end.

Give me a ring if you want to chat about it.

Regards as ever,

Linda O'Byrne
FICTION EDITOR

25-27 Camden Road · London NW1 9LL · Tel 071 284 0909 · Facsimile 071 485 3774
Partners: H. Bauer Publishing Limited. Heinrich Bauer Verlage Beteiligungsgesellschaft m.b.H

Fig. 12. Letter from Fiction Editor requesting alterations to manuscript.

Working through the manuscript again, I was able to rewrite the ending, bringing in an extra character in the shape of 'a large, plump man with a curly white beard' to introduce that vital 'hint of magic'.

Editorial changes were made to the title and the names of some of the characters and the edited story, which was initially submitted in July, was published in that year's Christmas issue of *Bella*.

As you can see, in the published version (see Fig. 13), the miserable old Santa, now called 'Mr Bleeze', is revealed to young Amy as a cheat. However, not only is her Christmas wish finally granted but the nasty 'Mr Bleeze' gets his come-uppance by being seen to present the local dignitary's daughter with a 'dirty rag doll'.

THE EVER-CHANGING MARKET

The women's magazine market is in a state of constant evolution. In order to appeal to as wide a readership as possible, each publication must adapt to the demands of a rapidly changing society.

As writers, it is up to us to reflect those changes in the lives, dialogue and actions of our characters. The ideas for stories are all around us. In our home, at work, in the supermarket, on the bus or taken from the media.

A good working knowledge of the magazine market and its target audience is vital. But perhaps the most essential ingredient is the ability to enjoy both writing and twisting a really good tale.

ASSIGNMENT

Select the magazines which you enjoy reading the most and study them carefully, comparing their content and styles.

Having clearly identified the issues they discuss and the topics they cover, continue to purchase the magazines on a regular basis to ensure that your stories will fit into their current formats.

Only submit one story at a time to each editor and don't be tempted to send the same story off to several different publications at once. Having the same story accepted by two editors can cause serious problems.

If your first few attempts are rejected, regard this as a learning experience and keep on trying. Success may be just around the next twist in the tale.

By Adele Ramet

Amy shivered with cold and pulled her cardigan tightly around her thin frame.

Hugging her battered teddy and pressing her nose against the rain-splashed window, she gazed longingly at the toys inside, piled high on Santa's sleigh. Most of all, she gazed at the doll sitting in splendour at the top of the pile. The doll had long blonde hair and a glittering pink and white dress.

"Shall we visit the fairy grotto, darling?"

Amy turned to watch a fond mother dragging a sulky faced boy into the department store.

'She could have asked me,' the little girl thought, shuddering as a large drip from the shop's awning found its way down her neck. 'Even if it isn't really Santa in that stupid grotto.'

A streetwise seven-year-old like Amy could tell the difference between bad-tempered Mr Bleeze — who frequented the local café where her mum worked — and the real Santa Claus.

"Clear off, you!" He'd chased her out of the grotto earlier that day. "You can't come in here unless you can pay and," he'd shifted his false belly triumphantly as he'd loomed over her, "I know your mum hasn't two pennies to rub together."

He'd pulled her to the grotto's glittering entrance. "Don't let me catch you here again or I'll set the coppers on you."

Amy shivered again as the rain turned to sleet and ran home as fast as she could. Dashing down a narrow alley, she fumbled for the key she wore around her neck, as she scrambled up the stairs into the bedsitter she shared with her mother.

"Will you take me to the fairy grotto at Markham's so I can send a special message to Santa?" Amy asked her mother at supper.

"What do you think?" It was more a sigh of resignation than a question. "Two pound fifty for ten seconds on that smarmy devil Bleeze's knee and a bit of

cheap, plastic rubbish. Don't be so stupid."

She set two plates of beans on the table. "And if you're thinking of asking for that fancy doll in Markham's window for Christmas, you can forget it."

Seeing the look in her daughter's eyes, her expression softened. "Eat your tea, love." A smile lit up her face and she patted Amy's hand. "Don't worry, Father Christmas will bring you something nice. He always knows what children want."

Amy sighed. How could he know without being told? She knew quite well that some presents came from her mum, but the big one always came from Santa. Why couldn't Mr Bleeze pass on a message?

"I've asked Mrs Clark downstairs to keep an eye on you again tomorrow while I'm working this overtime." Her mother's tone was extra bright. "So make sure you behave yourself."

Safe in the knowledge that Mrs Clark never took the slightest notice of her, Amy continued to visit Markham's every day, trying in vain to get into the grotto.

By Christmas Eve, she was desperate. As soon as her mother left for work, she hurried along to wait for Mr Bleeze at the staff entrance. She leapt out in front of him as he appeared. "Please will you give a message to Santa for me?"

"I thought I told you to stop hanging around." Breathing heavily, he bent down to glare at the child.

Stubbornly, Amy tried again. "I know Santa has asked you to pretend to be him, so he can get all his other work finished in time," she gabbled as fast as she could. "So the next time you speak to him, will you give him a message for me?"

Her voice tailed away as she saw the man begin to frown. "What on earth are you talking about? When I'm in that grotto, I am Father Christmas and I ain't givin' no messages to nobody."

He turned and stomped into the store. Amy quietly followed him through the door. At first, she was

worried that someone might see her, but she soon realised everyone was too busy to notice her.

"I want everything in perfect order before they arrive." A tall man in an immaculate suit was fussing over a display of leather handbags. "Lady Evelyn is sure to request a tour of all the departments."

Dodging between counters and elaborate display stands, Amy followed the man to the fairy grotto. "Bleeze!" He towered over Mr Bleeze as he struggled into his costume. "Is the box of toys ready?"

Amy was surprised to see

that Mr Bleeze looked frightened.

"Er, yes, sir, Mr Markham, sir." His hands shook as he fastened his beard. "I'll get it now." He squeezed himself behind a cardboard reindeer and emerged, hauling an enormous cardboard box behind him.

"Excellent. This appeal for used toys for underprivileged children has gone far better than I expected." He picked over the items at the top of the box. "Now don't forget, when you hand over the toys to Lady Evelyn, remember to give her one of our top-selling dolls for her

daughter! Wrap one up now in some pretty paper."

As soon as Mr Markham had left, Amy jumped out from her hiding place behind a giant teddy bear. "Mr Bleeze," she hissed. "Quick, before he comes back."

"What the hell?" Bleeze peered down. "Oh my gawd, who let you in? Right, my girl, this time it's the coppers!" He lunged at Amy and dragged her towards the manager's office.

Amy struggled free of his grasp. "Please, you've got to help me," she pleaded. "Just tell Santa I'd like the doll for Christmas."

Wiping her nose on her

shabby sleeve, she waited anxiously for his answer. Before he could reply, the store's speaker system crackled into life. "Attention, everyone! I am about to open the store. Lady Evelyn and the mayor will be arriving shortly."

"Oh no!" Mr Bleeze glared at Amy. "I've got to get rid of you quick. You want the doll, right?"

She nodded dumbly.

"If you get it, you'll clear off for good?"

"Yes!" she gasped, her eyes shining.

"Right." With his back to Amy, he quickly leant over

the box of old toys and fished out a large, homemade rag doll. It was a bit the worse for wear but, he reasoned, it was certainly the best the kid was likely to get.

Stuffing it into a Markham's carrier bag, he pushed it into the child's hands. "Now take this, go away and don't come back."

Amy rushed through the store, clutching the bag tightly to her chest. She swerved into a side aisle to avoid a large group of people who were sweeping through the main doors.

Not able to wait a second longer, she pulled open the bag. Disappointment cut through her like a knife as she stared at the dirty rag doll inside. Mr Bleeze had cheated and suddenly she realised with a cold chill in her stomach that Santa would never know now what she wanted for Christmas.

Frantic to get home, she began to run towards the main doors, only to find herself caught up in the rush of Christmas Eve shoppers coming in.

Still clutching the bag containing the hated doll, Amy bent her head and tried to ram a path through the crowd. She missed her footing and fell against a rack of jackets where she lay sobbing her heart out.

"Now then, my dear, what's all this?" A large, comforting hand stroked Amy's hair back from her wet eyes. "Are you hurt?"

Amy looked up to see a large, plump man with a curly white beard smiling down at her. "No, I'm all right." She scrambled to her feet, sniffing, remembering that she mustn't talk to strangers. "I've got to go."

She started towards the door but the man called her back. "Amy, you've forgotten something you wanted." He held out her carrier bag.

Snatching the bag from his hand, Amy ran out of the store. On the pavement, she pulled out the doll, determined to throw it in the nearest bin. Long blonde hair cascaded over her fingers, a swirl of pink and white glittered miraculously as she stood, transfixed.

"It's my doll," she breathed. "Santa got my message after all!"

Upstairs in the grotto, a bewildered Mr Bleeze was trying to explain to his apoplectic boss why he'd given Lady Evelyn a dirty rag doll for her daughter's Christmas present.

© Adele Ramet, 1990

Tell Santa

Fig. 13. Published version of *Bella* Mini Mystery 'Tell Santa'.

Tell Santa
by Adèle Ramet

Amy shivered with cold and pulled her cardigan tightly round her thin frame. Hugging her battered teddy and pressing her nose against the rain-splashed window, she gazed longingly at the toys inside, piled high on Santa's sleigh. Most of all, she gazed at the doll sitting in splendour at the top of the pile. The doll had long blonde hair and a glittering pink and white dress.

"Shall we visit the fairy grotto, darling?"

Amy turned to watch a fond mother dragging a sulky faced boy into the department store.

'She could have asked me,' the little girl thought, shuddering as a large drip from the shop's awning found its way down her neck. Even if it isn't really Santa in that stupid grotto.

A streetwise seven-year-old like Amy could tell the difference between bad-tempered Mr Bleeze – who frequented the local café where her mum worked – and the real Santa Claus.

"Clear off, you!" He'd chased her out of the grotto earlier that day. "You can't come in here unless you can pay and," he'd shifted his false belly triumphantly as he'd loomed over her. "I know your mum hasn't two pennies to rub together."

He'd pulled her to the grotto's glittering entrance. "Don't let me catch you here again or I'll set the coppers on you."

Amy shivered again as the rain turned to sleet and ran home as fast as she could. Splashing down a narrow alley, she fumbled for the key she wore around her neck, as she scrambled up the stairs to the bedsitter she shared with her mother.

"Will you take me to the fairy grotto at Markham's so I can send a special message to Santa?" Amy asked her mother at supper.

"What do you think?" It was more a sigh of resignation than a question. "Two pound fifty for ten seconds on that smarmy devil Bleeze's knee and a bit of cheap, plastic rubbish. Don't be so stupid."

She set two plates of beans on the table. "And if you're thinking of asking for that fancy doll in Markham's window for Christmas, you can forget it."

Seeing the look in her daughter's eyes, her expression softened. "Eat your tea, love." A smile lit up her face and she patted Amy's hand.

"Don't worry, Father Christmas will bring you something nice. He always knows what children want."

Amy sighed. How could he know without being told? She knew quite well that some presents came from her mum, but the big one always came from Santa. Why couldn't Mr Bleeze pass on a message?

"I've asked Mrs Clark downstairs to keep an eye on you again tomorrow while I'm working this overtime." Her mother's tone was extra bright. "So make sure you behave yourself."

Safe in the knowledge that Mrs Clark never took the slightest notice of her, Amy continued to visit Markham's every day, trying in vain to get into the grotto.

Fig. 14. Final manuscript accepted for publication.

By Christmas Eve, she was desperate. As soon as her mother left for work, she hurried along to wait for Mr Bleeze at the staff entrance. She leapt out in front of him as he appeared. "Please will you give a message to Santa for me?"

"I thought I told you to stop hanging around." Breathing heavily, he bent down to glare at the child.

Stubbornly, Amy tried again. "I know Santa has asked you to pretend to be him, so he can get all his other work finished in time," she gabbled as fast as she could. "So the next time you speak to him, will you give him a message for me?"

Her voice tailed away as she saw the man begin to frown. "What on earth are you talking about? When I'm in that grotto, I am Father Christmas and I ain't givin' no messages to nobody."

He turned and stomped into the store. Amy quietly followed him through the door. At first, she was worried that someone might see her, but she soon realised everyone was too busy to notice her.

"I want everything in perfect order before they arrive." A tall man in an immaculate suit was fussing over a display of leather handbags. "Lady Evelyn is sure to request a tour of all the departments."

Dodging between counters and elaborate display stands, Amy followed the man to the fairy grotto.

"Bleeze!" He towered over Mr Bleeze as he struggled into his costume. "Is the box of toys ready?"

Amy was surprised to see that Mr Bleeze looked frightened.

"Er, yes, sir, Mr Markham, sir." His hands shook as he fastened his beard. "I'll get it now." He squeezed himself behind a cardboard reindeer and emerged, hauling an enormous cardboard box behind him.

"Excellent. This appeal for used toys for underprivileged children has gone far better than I expected." He picked over the items at the top of the box. "Now don't forget, when you hand over the toys to Lady Evelyn, remember to give her one of our top-selling dolls for her daughter! Wrap one up now in some pretty paper."

As soon as Mr Markham had left, Amy jumped out from her hiding place behind a giant teddy bear. "Mr Bleeze," she hissed. "Quick, before he comes back."

"What the hell?" Bleeze peered down. "Oh my gawd, who let you in? Right, my girl, this time it's the coppers!" He lunged at Amy and dragged her towards the manager's office.

Amy struggled free of his grasp. "Please, you've got to help me," she pleaded. "Just tell Santa I'd like the doll for Christmas."

Wiping her nose on her shabby sleeve, she waited anxiously for his answer. Before he could reply, the store's speaker system crackled into life. "Attention, everyone! I am about to open the store. Lady Evelyn and the mayor will be arriving shortly."

"Oh no!" Mr Bleeze glared at Amy. "I've got to get rid of you quick. You want the doll, right?"

She nodded dumbly.

"If you get it, you'll clear off for good?"

"Yes!" she gasped, her eyes shining.

"Right." With his back to Amy, he quickly leant over the box of old toys and fished out a large, homemade rag doll. It was a bit worse for wear but, he reasoned, it was certainly the best the kid was likely to get.

Stuffing it into a Markham's carrier bag, he pushed it into the child's hands. "Now take this, go away and don't come back."

Amy rushed through the store, clutching the bag tightly to her chest. She swerved into a side aisle to avoid a large group of people who were sweeping through the main doors.

Not able to wait a second longer, she pulled open the bag. Disappointment cut through her like a knife as she stared at the dirty rag doll inside. Mr Bleeze had cheated and suddenly she realised with a cold chill in her stomach that Santa would never know now what she wanted for Christmas.

Frantic to get home, she began to run towards the main doors, only to find herself caught up in the rush of Christmas Eve shoppers coming in.

Still clutching the bag containing the hated doll, Amy bent her head and tried to ram a path through the crowd. She missed her footing and fell against a rack of jackets where she lay sobbing her heart out.

"Now then, my dear, what's all this?" A large, comforting hand stroked Amy's hair back from her wet eyes. "Are you hurt?"

Amy looked up to see a large, plump man with a curly white beard smiling down at her. "No, I'm all right." She scrambled to her feet, sniffing, remembering that she mustn't talk to strangers. "I've got to go."

She started towards the door but the man called her back. "Amy, you've forgotten something you wanted." He held out her carrier bag.

Snatching the bag from his hand, Amy ran out of the store. On the pavement, she pulled out the doll, determined to throw it in the nearest bin. Long blonde hair cascaded over her fingers, a swirl of pink and white glittered miraculously as she stood transfixed.

"It's my doll," she breathed. "Santa got my message after all!"

Upstairs in the grotto, a bewildered Mr Bleeze was trying to explain to his apoplectic boss why he'd given Lady Evelyn a dirty rag doll for her daughter's Christmas present.

© Adèle Ramet, 1990

Answers to Assignments

HIDDEN MEANINGS *(p. 46)*

1. (b)   An actor on stage
2. (b)   A surgeon sewing up a patient
3. (b)   An old lady
4. (b)   A man trying on clothes in a trendy menswear shop

CUTTING AND TIGHTENING *(p. 84)*

Terrified, he pressed his foot harder on the brake. Nothing! Gathering speed, the car hurtled down the mountainside towards a tortuous bend in the road.

(25 words)

PUNCTUATION *(p. 99)*

Julie awoke late the following morning, 'Oh no!' she cried, as she leapt out of bed and rushed downstairs into the kitchen, 'I'll lose my job if I miss the bus. For Heaven's sake, Mum, why didn't you wake me?'

Calmly, her mother carried on sipping her tea, 'I'd forget about breakfast if I were you,' she bit into a slice of thickly buttered toast, 'It's too late for that but if you're quick, you might have time for a shower.

'You did this deliberately,' Julie snapped as she hurried towards the bathroom.

'Did what?' her mother raised an innocent eyebrow, 'It's hardly my fault if you don't get up when your alarm goes off. Personally, I don't know how anyone could sleep through that racket. I would have thought its bell was loud enough to waken the dead.'

Glossary

Central character The character whose story you are telling.

Chase-up letter Brief note to an editor requesting a decision on your story.

Commission A story written at the request of an editor to specified requirements and for an agreed fee.

Conflict Problems and emotions which provide the obstacles the central character has to overcome.

Copyright The legal ownership of publication rights in a piece of written work.

Covering letter Brief note to an editor requesting consideration of your story.

Cutting and tightening Editing your story to length and style so that it flows smoothly.

Dialect An accent and vocabulary peculiar to a specific region.

Dialogue Direct speech between two or more characters.

Double-line spacing Leaving a blank line between each typewritten line on a page.

Editor The person responsible for purchasing a story and reproducing it in the magazine.

Editorial guidelines Information for freelance writers regarding the magazine's editorial requirements.

Flashback A method of revealing background through snippets of information.

Format The style and content of a magazine.

Front sheet A sheet of paper at the front of a manuscript bearing the name and address of the author and the title of the story.

Genre The literary category into which a story fits.

Illusion story A story in which the characters are not who they appear to be.

Interaction The way characters react to the people, settings and objects around them.

International Reply Coupon A method of payment to cover postage costs from foreign countries to the UK.

Invoice A statement of account requesting payment of the agreed sum for a manuscript.

Kill-fee A sum of money agreed with an editor in payment for a manuscript which has been retained for a considerable length of time on a 'payment on publication' basis but is unlikely to be published in the foreseeable future.

Lead time The deadline for submitting manuscripts aimed at specific dates or seasons.

Payment slip Notification from a publisher detailing the amount paid to an author and the copyright purchased.

Plot The plan of events running through a story.

Protagonist The main character.

Reader identification Characters and settings immediately recognisable to the magazine's readership.

Revamp Giving a magazine a new format.

Short story A work of fiction of less than 10,000 words.

Signpost A clue which moves the action of the story forward.

Slush pile Collection of unsolicited manuscripts submitted to an editor.

Stereotype A fixed image of specific groups based on age, sex, race, religion or social status.

Storyline The theme of a story.

Syndication To offer stories for sale to magazines worldwide for simultaneous publication.

Targeting Researching and producing work in a specific market style.

Unsolicited manuscript A story submitted unrequested to an editor.

Viewpoint The point of view from which a story is told.

Viewpoint character The character from whose point of view the story is told.

Wordage The number of words in which the story must be told in order to fit a specific slot.

Useful Addresses

ASSOCIATIONS

National Union of Journalists, Acorn House, 314–320 Gray's Inn Road, London WC1X 8DP. Tel: (0171) 278 7916.

Society of Authors, 84 Drayton Gardens, London SW10 9SB. Tel: (0171) 373 6642.

Society of Women Writers & Journalists, 110 Whitehall Road, Chingford, London E4 6DW. Tel: (0181) 529 0886.

South Eastern Writers' Association, Secretary, 8 Beaumont Close, Gidea Park, Romford, Essex RM2 6LJ. Tel: (01708) 742009.

Women Writers' Network, 55 Burlington Lane, London W4 3ET. Tel: (0181) 994 0598.

Writers' Guild of Great Britain, 430 Edgware Road, London W2 1EH. Tel: (0171) 723 8074–5–6.

UK WEEKLY MAGAZINES

Bella, 25–27 Camden Road, London NW1 9LL. Tel: (0171) 284 0909 (switchboard).

Best, G & J of the UK, Portland House, Stag Place, London SW1E 5AB. Tel: (0171) 245 8833.

Chat, IPC Magazines, King's Reach Tower, Stamford Street, London SE1 9LS. Tel: (0171) 261 5000 (switchboard).

My Weekly, D. C. Thomson & Co. Ltd., 80 Kingsway East, Dundee DD4 8SL. Tel: (01382) 223 131.

Take A Break, H. Bauer Publishing, 25–27 Camden Road, London NW1 9LL. Tel: (0171) 284 0909 (switchboard).

That's Life! H. Bauer Publishing, 7th Floor, 140 Tottenham Court Road, London W1 9LN. Tel: (0171) 388 6269.

The Lady, 39–40 Bedford Street, London WC2E 9ER. Tel: (0171) 379 4717.

Woman, IPC Magazines, King's Reach Tower, Stamford Street, London SE1 9LS. Tel: (0171) 261 5000 (switchboard).

Woman & Home, IPC Magazines, King's Reach Tower, Stamford Street, London SE1 9LS. Tel: (0171) 261 5000 (switchboard).

Woman's Realm, IPC Magazines, King's Reach Tower, Stamford Street, London SE1 9LS. Tel: (0171) 261 5000 (switchboard).

Woman's Weekly, IPC Magazines, King's Reach Tower, Stamford Street, London SE1 9LS. Tel: (0171) 261 5000 (switchboard).

Yours, Choice Publications, Apex House, Oundle Road, Peterborough PE2 9NP. Tel: (01733) 555123.

Useful Reading

Roget's Thesaurus, Penguin Books.
The Writers' Handbook, Macmillan.
Writers' & Artists' Yearbook, A & C Black.
Writers' Monthly, 29 Turnpike Lane, London N8 0EP.
Writers' News, PO Box 4, Nairn IV12 4HU.
How to Write Stories for Magazines, Donna Baker, Allison & Busby.
The Magazine Writer's Handbook, Gordon Wells, Allison & Busby.
The Writer's Digest Handbook of Short Story Writing.
Writing for Magazines, Jill Dick, A & C Black.
Writing for the Market, Patricia O'Reilly, Mercier Press.
Writing Popular Fiction, Rona Randall, A & C Black.

HOW TO BOOKS in this series
How to Write & Sell A Novel, Marina Oliver.
Starting to Write, Marina & Deborah Oliver.
Copyright & Law for Writers, Helen Shay.
How to Write for Publication, Chriss McCallum.
How to Write for Television, William Smethurst.

Index

COPYRIGHT & LAW FOR WRITERS
How to protect yourself and your creative work

Helen Shay

This book will be a useful tool for any writer, but especially invaluable to beginners and those just starting to enjoy some success. Make sure you never receive any legal short change. This book takes you through the main legal implications relevant to writers, from first putting pen to paper/finger to keyboard through to selling work, entering a contract and onto collecting the full financial rewards due to you. It also explains exactly what to do if things go wrong. It explains the various pitfalls and how to steer clear of them – for example copyright infringement – whilst showing how to preserve your own rights, and learning how to publish and not be damned. A graduate of Manchester University, Helen Shay is a qualified solicitor of twelve years' standing. Currently working in an ombudsman's office in London, she is well-versed in the problems which can confront the individual versus large organisations. She also tutors and lectures part-time in business law. She is a member of the Society of Women Writers and Journalists and the Women Writers Network, and currently writes a regular legal column for *Writers News*.

160pp. illus. 1 85703 416 3.

WRITING A NONFICTION BOOK
How to prepare your work for publication

Norman Toulson

'At least you don't have to dream up a plot.' No, but you need to seize and hold your readers' attention as firmly as the author of a whodunnit. In this book Norman Toulson guides the would-be author along the road from ambition to publication. He describes how to collect facts and figures, and plan your information in chapters. He tells you how to find a publisher and sell your concept of the book to him. He shows how you can breathe life into your draft and polish it until it shines. He adds how you can co-operate with the publisher to turn your manuscript into a book and sell it to the public. Norman Toulson has had seven non-fiction books published. They deal with various topics. One evoked the comment, 'I never knew the history of an insurance company could be so enthralling.'

160pp. illus. 1 85703 426 0.

HOW TO WRITE FOR TELEVISION
A complete guide to writing and marketing TV scripts

William Smethurst

Television is a huge and expanding market for the freelance writer. Particularly in the field of drama, producers are constantly looking for new writers for situation comedies, series drama, and soap operas and single plays. But what kind of scripts are required? How should a script be presented and laid out? What camera moves should you put in, and should you plan for commercial breaks? Which programmes and organisations should you contact, and which are the subjects to tackle or avoid? Packed with hard-hitting information and advice, and illustrated throughout with examples, this is a complete step-by-step manual for every writer wanting to break into this lucrative market. 'Packed with information which is well presented and easily accessible.' *National Association of Careers & Guidance Teachers Bulletin.* 'If would be TV scriptwriters are looking for a wide ranging and practical book to light the fuse which could lead to a successful career, they should certainly invest in a copy of William Smethurst's *How to Write for Television.*' *BAFTA News.* 'Your best starting point is probably William Smethurst's book.' *Writers News.* William Smethurst has written numerous scripts for both radio and television. He has been a television script editor at BBC Pebble Mill, and executive producer of drama serials for Central Television. He is now a director of the Independent television company, Andromeda Television Ltd.

160pp illus. 1 85703 045 1.

STARTING TO WRITE
How to create written work for publication and profit

Marina & Deborah Oliver

How does a writer get started? How do writers manage the physical aspects? This new book shows would-be writers how to look at their motives, how to set realistic objectives, and how to devise a plan of action without wasting time and resources. Illustrated throughout with case studies, it will show you how to explore various options, discover what methods work best for you, and take advantage of tips from experienced writers. Start now, and learn how to get your work into print. Marina Oliver has written and published over 30 novels, published her own magazine, written and edited many booklets, and taught creative writing. Deborah Oliver has edited a monthly magazine and is currently production editor of a computer magazine.

128pp. illus. 1 85703 401 5.

HOW TO WRITE FOR PUBLICATION
Your practical guide to success

Chriss McCallum

'How can I sell my work? How do I protect my copyright? Can a magazine steal my story? Why just a printed rejection slip – can't editors tell me where I'm going wrong? Are writing courses worth the money? Should I get an agent?' Highly expert and practical, *How to Write for Publication* gives the often surprising answers to these and hundreds of other questions most often asked by the great silent majority of struggling writers, whether of fiction, nonfiction, poetry, drama, stories or articles. No author seriously interested in getting published can afford to be without this manual, packed with checklists, examples and key contacts. 'Handy for both professional and newcomer alike.' *Writers News.* 'Everything you ever wanted to know about the practical side of publishing . . . excellent.' *Competitors Journal.* 'Really definitive . . . Leaves every other similar book in its shade.' *Pause (National Poetry Foundation).* 'It is, quite simply one of the best books of its kind that I've ever read.' Steve Wetton, Author of BBC TV's comedy drama *Growing Pains.* 'The revised edition maintains the high standard . . . Its reference section of useful addresses is value for money on its own.' *Writers News.* Chriss McCallum has many years' experience as a professional Editor, and has worked for Collins, Penguin, W H Allen and other leading firms. She was publisher of *The Writers Voice* (1983-86) and is a Member of the Society of Authors, The Society of Women Writers & Journalists, and an Honorary Member of the Comedy Writers Association.

192pp. illus. 1 85703 140 7. 3rd edition.

WRITING & SELLING SHORT STORIES
How to get your creative work into print

Daphne Moss

This is an up-to-date, practical, and revelatory book on how to write short stories that sell. It teaches not only writing techniques but also how to present your work, to find the right markets, and reveals what today's editors are looking for in a short story. It is a guide to everything you want to know, from the moment you get your first idea, through the writing and polishing, to when you send out an invoice for the story you've sold. Daphne Moss has been a writer and broadcaster for over twenty years. Her work has appeared in magazines and newspapers both in the UK and abroad. She tutors Creative Writing classes, has written booklets and gives talks on all aspects of writing, and is Chairman of the Society of Women Writers & Journalists.

160pp. illus. 1 85703 421 X.

CREATIVE WRITING
How to develop your writing skills for successful fiction and non-fiction work

Adèle Ramet

The term 'Creative Writing' covers a broad spectrum of skills from writing non-fiction articles and features for specialist magazines to romantic fiction, ghost stories and crime novels. This book guides you through key techniques, with exercises aimed at helping you to write more effectively in your chosen genre. You will be encouraged to approach your work from different angles, demonstrating how to bring a fresh slant to non-fiction pieces and how to involve yourself more fully in the lives of your fictional characters. Whatever your writing interest, this book will help you write more creatively and lead you further along the route towards publication. Adèle Ramet is Chairman of the South Eastern Writers Association and an experienced writing tutor. She has contributed widely to *Bella*, *Woman's Realm*, and many other leading women's magazines.

144pp. illus. 1 85703 451 1.

WRITING & SELLING A NOVEL
How to craft your fiction for publication

Marina Oliver

Writing a novel seems a daunting task until attempted. Marina Oliver's invaluable, eminently practical book, based on firsthand experience, offers realistic encouragement, down to earth advice, expert tips and suggestions to guide aspiring novelists. They include how to get started, the key elements to consider, where to look for help, how to approach publishers and what to expect during the process of publication. A former further education lecturer, and tutor for creative writing courses, Marina Oliver has published over 30 novels, short, long, historical and contemporary. Chairman of the Romantic Novelists' Association 1991-3, and an adviser to the 1994 edition of the biographical dictionary, *Twentieth Century Romance* and *Historical Writers*, she lectures widely on writing.

144pp. illus. 1 85703 406 6.